This book is dedicated to our

daughter Jill Biggs Tumminello.

I love you very much and I am so proud

of the wonderful young woman you have become.

◀ **Inside front cover: Occupancy in the new AAA-Mid-Atlantic building on the Christina
(right, on the river), a project of The Commonwealth Group, was slated for summer 2005.
Christina Landing, the high-rise, luxury apartment building and town-homes on the south side
of the river, a Buccini/Pollen project, is scheduled to open in fall 2005.**

MILLER PUBLISHING, INC.
1201 N. Orange Street, Suite 200
Wilmington, DE 19801
www.millerpublishinginc.com
fmiller2@dscc.com

Published in 2005
Printed in Korea

Library of Congress Control Number 2004117416
ISBN: 0-9663337-2-1
First Edition October 2005

Photography: Mike Biggs
www.mikebiggsphotography.com
Text: Lise Monty
Design Direction/Production: Simpson Studio, Inc.
Design Corporate Profiles: PKM Design
Publisher: Frederick Miller

Wilmington...
On the Move

A sleek Amtrak Acela arrives at the historic Wilmington Train Station.

Photography by Mike Biggs/Text by Lise Monty

Designed by Simpson Studio, Inc.

Published by Miller Publishing, Inc.
Wilmington, Delaware

This book was made possible through the generosity of the following...

City of Wilmington
Delaware State Chamber of Commerce
Daisy Construction Company
Diamond Technologies, Inc.
Port of Wilmington/Diamond State Port Corporation
Citrosuco North America Inc.
Murphy Marine Services, Inc.
M. Davis & Sons, Inc.
The Buccini/Pollin Group, Inc.
Hercules, Inc.
St. Francis Healthcare Services
CAI
The Commonwealth Group
Wilmington College
Jackson Cross Partners, LLC
Cover & Rossiter, P.A.
Christiana Care Health System
Emory Hill Real Estate Services, Inc.
University of Delaware
Blue Cross Blue Shield of Delaware
The Hotel du Pont
AAA Mid-Atlantic
Gilbane
AstraZeneca Pharmaceuticals, Inc.
Wilmington Blue Rocks LP
Delaware Technical & Community College
Delaware River & Bay Authority

Contents

Foreword

Cities change – and the people who live and work in the city can control that change.

As I come to work at the Government Center each morning, and as I visit Wilmington's businesses, neighborhoods, community centers, and parks every day, I see striking evidence of how change is occurring in Delaware's largest city and how our citizens are making it happen.

A decade ago, development of the Christina Riverfront was about 90 percent dream and 10 percent reality. Frawley Stadium and the Riverfront Arts Center were brand new, but there was little other than aging warehouses and empty shells on the one-mile path from the stadium to the Amtrak Station. Now the Riverfront is getting livelier – and lovelier –by the day. It is home to ING Direct and Juniper Bank, the Delaware Theater Company, the Delaware Center for the Contemporary Arts, AAA Mid-Atlantic, restaurants that appeal to every taste and wallet, Tubman-Garrett Park and the relaxing Riverwalk. The Russell W. Peterson Urban Wildlife Refuge is being developed; a hotel and luxury high-rise housing are on the drawing boards.

Aging buildings near Second and Market Streets have been transformed into the Ships Tavern District, an eclectic blend of office, retail, and residential space. On the east side of Market Street, a parking garage with more than 15,000 square feet of retail space will complete the Christina Gateway complex.

Look downtown, and see more change. The DuPont Company still stands tall, but the banking industry, led by MBNA, now has a commanding presence in the blocks around Rodney Square. There is new residential life – and a commitment to downtown living – in two strategically located, former office high-rises. Signs of Wilmington's enduring love of the arts continue to appear – the new Theatre N and the Baby Grand complement the DuPont Theatre and the Grand Opera House. Our downtown has also become a thriving educational center, with the Delaware College of Art and Design, Drexel University, and Springfield College joining more established branches of Delaware Technical & Community College, the University of Delaware, Delaware State University, and Wilmington College.

Residential areas are experiencing change too. Just a few blocks east of Rodney Square are several attractive new communities, including McCaulley Court and Kirkwood Manor. Off Northeast Boulevard, the Wilmington Housing Authority and Leon N. Weiner & Associates leveled an aging, drug-infested public housing complex and restored hope for residents of the townhouses in the new Village of Eastlake.

Yes, as I travel throughout Wilmington, I see a city in the midst of change. And I see business leaders, government officials, community organizers and ordinary citizens working together to make good things happen.

We are seeing a new Wilmington emerging from the old. The pace need not be fast, but it must be steady; it must be persistent; it must be relentless. Person by person, block by block, business by business, neighborhood by neighborhood, some of the greatest advances in our City's history are now being realized. There can be no doubt that Wilmington has begun to experience a rebirth that many thought impossible just a few years ago.

Beneficial partnerships among the City, County, State and Federal governments, as well as with the private sector, community organizations, and churches, have resulted in greater economic growth, new housing developments, neighborhood improvements, and better parks, streets, and transportation. Collaborations involving the Riverfront Development Corporation, Wilmington Renaissance Corporation, and the Christina Gateway Corporation have accelerated our City's transformation.

We are continuing to renew our neighborhoods. The Wilmington Housing Partnership has already created 2,500 homeownership opportunities, acquired vacant and blighted housing units, demolished or rehabilitated vacant properties, and funded housing counseling programs. It is now stabilizing neighborhoods that are at risk of deterioration, working with neighborhood organizations to build community pride, and finding the resources to build or rehabilitate 150 houses so more Wilmington residents may realize the dream of homeownership.

We have made enormous progress because we have the energy, the will, the innovation, and the intelligence to reach our goals. Where we go from here will depend on our resources, both financial and human, and our vision.

Our vision requires a commitment to build upon the successes we have already achieved. Development of the Atrium at the Amtrak Station and the Renaissance Center at Fourth and King Streets will extend the revitalization already occurring on the Riverfront and in the Ships Tavern District. Strengthening the Shipley Street corridor will establish another link between the Rodney Square area and the new vibrant areas near Martin Luther King Boulevard. Projects on the south and east banks of the Christina, some underway and others being planned, demonstrate the commitment of both the public and private sectors to maximize the riverfront's potential.

The vision of the new Wilmington extends upward, as well. For some bold thinkers, our future includes elevated parkland forming a deck over Interstate 95 between the Trinity Vicinity and Cool Spring neighborhoods. Is it merely a dream to seek to reconnect a City that was divided by an Interstate highway? Or is it a visionary concept that symbolizes Wilmington's hope, its energy, and its courage?

As you enjoy this book, with its photographs of our beautiful and vibrant City, take a moment to reflect upon our accomplishments. Then imagine the future, as I do, and envision the images that will be included in another volume, a generation from now.

Remember, not many years ago, there were more than a few people who doubted our riverfront could ever be revived. The imagination and perseverance of the people of Wilmington helped prove the naysayers wrong. And today we will look to the future with the confidence that Wilmington will continue to grow and prosper.

Mayor James M. Baker

The Federal-style Old Town Hall, built in 1798, housed the city's meeting chambers, offices and jail. It was also the center of political and social activities during a period when Wilmington's milling industries and its port prospered. The death of George Washington was observed there in 1799, as were receptions and dinners for the Marquis de Lafayette and President Andrew Jackson. Henry Clay's body was laid in state there in 1851. Restored to its classical beauty, it now provides space for exhibitions, programs and special events presented by the Historical Society of Delaware, whose period archway spreads over Market Street Mall. ▶

History

Walker's Mill, where cotton and woolen goods were produced from 1815 to the late 1930s, chills out on the banks of the Brandywine just downstream from Hagley Museum.

Wilmington — The First Four Centuries

16th Century –The peace-loving Lenni Lenape Indians, Delaware's first citizens, live here and throughout an area extending north to what is now New York City.

1638 – A group of Swedes and Finns sail on the *Kalmar Nyckel* up the Delaware River into a smaller river they name the Christina after their young queen. They establish Fort Christina, the first permanent European settlement in what is now Wilmington. Fort Christina State Park perpetuates the memory of these first settlers and preserves "The Rocks" where they first landed. Adjacent to the park is an operational historical shipyard created to build a replica of the *Kalmar Nyckel,* which was launched in 1997 and retains a high profile as Delaware's Tall Ship.

1638 – The settlers in New Sweden introduce the construction of log houses to the New World.

1639 – The first African on the Delaware, Black Anthony, is brought from the Caribbean to Fort Christina.

1643 – Johan Printz becomes governor of New Sweden. A huge man weighing nearly 400 pounds, Governor Printz keeps the little colony going for 11 years despite considerable adversity.

1651 – Gov. Peter Stuyvesant of New Netherland (now New York and New Jersey) builds Fort Casimir just a few miles south of Fort Christina.

1655 – The Dutch defeat the Swedes on the Delaware, ending the New Sweden Colony.

1664 – The English seize the Dutch settlements and claim the land for James, Duke of York. Delaware becomes an English colony.

1673 – The Dutch regain control of the Delaware.

1674 – The English regain the Delaware.

1682 – The Duke of York transfers control of the Delaware Colony to English Quaker William Penn, who just founded the colony of Pennsylvania.

1698 – Descendants of the first Swedish colony in Wilmington build Holy Trinity Church, affectionately known as "Old Swedes." It flourishes today as the nation's oldest church building still standing as originally built and is still in regular use for worship. Among those buried in the church yard are three members of a distinguished Delaware family: James Bayard, Senator; Richard Bayard, first Mayor of Wilmington; and Thomas F. Bayard, Secretary of State under President Cleveland and later Ambassador to the Court of St. James.

1731 – Thomas Willing founds a town on the banks of the Christina River which he calls Willingtown. He lays out the streets in a grid pattern, just as they are in Philadelphia. He puts the lots up for sale, but virtually no one is interested.

1735 – William Shipley of Philadelphia buys land in Willingtown, recognizing its potential for trade with the Christina River making a good harbor.

1739 – About 600 people live in Willingtown in newly constructed houses of brick and wood.

1739 – The Penn family gives Willingtown a charter and renames it Wilmington, in honor of the Earl of Wilmington, an important English official.

1742-1760s – Flour mills run by Quakers flourish on the banks of the Brandywine. Wheat purchased from area farmers is ground into flour and sent to market in the West Indies and Europe. Trade keeps expanding and so does the population, now close to 2000.

1761 – James Adams sets up the first printing press in Delaware at Wilmington.

1776 – **July 1-2** – Caesar Rodney makes heroic overnight ride to Philadelphia to cast the vote that put Delaware on the side of independence. An iconic statue in Wilmington's Rodney Square immortalizes the patriot's historic ride.

1777 – British occupy Wilmington after winning the Battle of the Brandywine.

1787 – Delaware is the first state to ratify the new U.S. Constitution – on December 7.

1788-89 – Abolition societies are established in Wilmington and Dover.

1795 – Bank of Delaware, the state's first bank, is founded in Wilmington.

1802 – Eleuthère Irénee du Pont de Nemours begins manufacturing gunpowder on 95 acres of land along the Brandywine Creek, laying the foundation of the DuPont Company.

1814 – August Quarterly is started by Peter Spencer, founder of African Union Methodist Protest Church in Wilmington. America's first major black religious festival continues in the 21st century.

1838 – The Philadelphia, Wilmington and Baltimore Railroad begins carrying passengers from Wilmington to Philadelphia and Baltimore.

1844 – *The Bangor,* America's first iron-hulled propeller steamship, is launched in Wilmington.

1861-65 – War breaks out between the United States and the Confederate States. About 12,000 men from Delaware join the Union Army, about 500 join the Confederate Army.

1878 – First telephone line is installed in Wilmington.

1882 – First electric street lights are installed in Wilmington.

1887 – *Volunteer,* a steel-hulled racing yacht built in Wilmington, defeats *Thistle* to win America's Cup.

1888 – Electric street cars begin to replace horse cars in Wilmington.

1899 – The Delaware Corporation Law is passed making it easier for businesses to incorporate in Delaware than in other states. Today, 300,000 companies, including 58 percent of the Fortune 500, are incorporated in Delaware.

1900 – Illustrator Howard Pyle opens his art school in Wilmington. N.C. Wyeth is a student.

1913 – Hotel du Pont and the Playhouse open.

1913 – Wilson Line ferry begins ferry service between Wilmington and Pennsville, N.J.

1917-18 – Nearly 10,000 Delawareans serve in World War 1.

1921-23 – Wilmington Marine Terminal is constructed.

1934 – U.S. Supreme Court confirms Delaware's claim to control the Delaware River.

1937 – Wallace H. Carothers, leading a DuPont Co. synthetic polymers research team working at the company's Experimental Station, invents nylon.

1938 – President Franklin D. Roosevelt and Delaware dignitaries dedicate a monument in honor of the *Kalmar Nyckel* in a small park at "The Rocks." Fashioned from Swedish black granite and celebrating the 300th anniversary of the first Swedish settlement in Delaware, the handsome monument still anchors the river end of Fort Christina State Park.

1941-45 – 30,000 Delaware men and women serve in armed forces in World War II. At home, more than 10,000 people are employed building ships and military landing craft that helped win the war.

1951 – Delaware Memorial Bridge opens first span linking Delaware to New Jersey.

1951 – Henry Francis du Pont, great-grandson of the DuPont Co. founder, opens his garden and extensive decorative arts collection as Winterthur Museum, Library and Gardens.

1952 – Chancellor Collins J. Seitz deems Delaware's segregated schools to be separate and unequal, a position upheld by the U.S. Supreme Court in *Brown v. Board of Education*. Judge Seitz is the nation's first judge to order segregated schools to admit black students.

1963 – President John F. Kennedy opens Delaware Turnpike (I-95) in one of his last public appearances.

1968 – Riots break out in Wilmington following the assassination of Martin Luther King, Jr., prompting a 10-month occupation of the city by National Guard, the longest occupation in the country.

1971 – The Delaware Coastal Zone Act, which limits heavy industry in wetlands and marshes along Delaware River, becomes law.

1975 – William "Judy" Johnson, a former Negro League baseball player, becomes the state's first player elected to the National Baseball Hall of Fame.

1976 – The restored Grand Opera House opens as Delaware's Center for the Performing Arts.

1981 – The Delaware State Legislature passes the Financial Center Development Act, giving credit-card banks the freedom to set interest rates and a big incentive to set up business in Delaware. More than 30 out-of-state banks move their headquarters to Delaware.

2000 – Ruth Ann Minner is elected Delaware's first woman governor.

2002 – The Clean Air Act, which bans smoking in public places, becomes law.

2004 – James M. Baker is re-elected mayor of Wilmington in a landslide.
　　　Ruth Ann Minner is re-elected governor of Delaware.

More than 800 students in academic and career-training programs attend Howard High School of Technology located just three blocks from Wilmington's thriving downtown business area. The school's state-of-the-art computer technology lab offers students a wide variety of programs, from skill reinforcement and SAT preparation to word processing and desktop publishing. Howard is the only high school in Delaware, and the second in the nation, to offer a Microsoft-based computer systems engineering program of study. It is the winner of a Superstars in Education award for the "Quest of Quality" given by the Delaware State Chamber of Commerce. Built in 1927, the once-segregated school, recognized for its role in educating thousands of black Delawareans who became prominent, has been designated a National Historic Landmark. ▶

In 1698-99, descendants of Delaware's first European colony, primarily Swedish, built Holy Trinity Church with Brandywine granite. Affectionately known as Old Swedes, it was established as a Swedish Lutheran Church then in 1971 transferred to the Episcopal church. Today it is recognized as one of the country's oldest church buildings still in regular use for worship. Among those buried here are three members of a distinguished Delaware family: James Bayard, Senator; Richard Bayard, first Mayor of Wilmington; and Thomas F. Bayard, Secretary of State under President Cleveland and later Ambassador to the Court of St. James.

Settlers of the New Sweden Colony introduced log house construction into America after they settled here in 1638, as memorialized today in Fort Christina State Park by this cabin moved from its original site near Price's Corner. The handsome black-granite monument (left), topped by a replica of the Kalmar Nyckel, was a 1938 gift from the people of Sweden celebrating the 300th anniversary of the first Swedish settlement in Delaware. It stands in a small park at "The Rocks," marking the exact spot where the Swedes landed.

Delaware's Tall Ship, the Kalmar Nyckel, serves as the state's goodwill ambassador at festivals and other events in Baltimore, Philadelphia and Norfolk, Virginia, among other cities. Built by volunteers who launched it in 1997, the modern-day beauty is a replica of the ship that in 1638 brought Wilmington's first settlers from Sweden and Finland. They sailed up the Delaware River into a smaller river they named the Christina for their young queen.

When it was founded in 1798, Brandywine Academy (right) on Vandever Street in historic Brandywine Village had one room on each floor for classes or meetings. In 1824, residents rang the Academy bell to greet a celebrity of the day, the Marquis de Lafayette, when he rode through the Village. The French general, who joined George Washington's army during the American Revolution, had returned to the United States for a tour and basked in welcoming crowds wherever he went. In 1839 Methodist women started a Sunday school in the building for children who worked in the nearby flour mills powered by the Brandywine River. Over the years, it has served as a social center, place of worship, public library, clubhouse and polling place. Today it is the home of AIA Delaware, which renovated the building in 2001. Various organizations occupy several of Brandywine Village's former homes on Market Street (above).

FOUNDED
1798

BRANDYWINE ACADEMY
Built 1798

Six historic houses, dating from 1748 to the early 1800s, make up Willingtown Square, a part of the Historical Society of Delaware's campus in downtown Wilmington. The houses were built when mercantile and shipping activities were prevalent along the Christina River and grain mills lined the banks of the Brandywine. The buildings were moved in 1976 from various sites throughout Wilmington to the 500 block of Market Street. Willingtown Square is named after Thomas Willing who in 1731 laid out the village that was to become the city of Wilmington. The buildings can be viewed from the outside but are not open to the public.

John Dickinson, lawyer, scholar, statesman and signer of the U.S. Constitution, and Thomas Garrett, famous abolitionist and friend of Harriet Tubman, are among many of the city's former leaders buried at Wilmington Friends Meeting. Located at Fourth and West Streets, the unadorned brick structure was completed in 1817. It stands as a tribute to the many Quakers who were effective leaders in establishing Wilmington as a vibrant city.

Sculptor James Edward Kelly captures the drama of Caesar Rodney's famous ride in this equestrienne statue that looms over Rodney Square, the public center of downtown Wilmington. On the stormy night of July 1, 1776, Rodney rode all night from Dover to Philadelphia to swing Delaware's vote at the 2nd Continental Congress in favor of U.S. independence. A likeness of the statue is imprinted on the state's commemorative quarters issued by the U.S. Mint. The statue and square date to the 1920s. On the square are headquarters for MBNA (center), the state's largest private-sector employer, and Wilmington Trust. MBNA owns the former courthouse in the background. Not shown are DuPont Company headquarters and the Wilmington Institute Free Library. ▶

When it opened in 1868 at Ninth and Washington Streets, Grace Church was the largest church in the city. Its construction celebrated the first century of Methodism in Wilmington and the Union victory in Gettysburg, which saved the city from the possibility of invasion by Confederate troops. Built in a modified Gothic style with distinctive green serpentine stone taken from quarries in Chadds Ford, Pennsylvania, it has always been a downtown landmark. Today, the United Methodist church has more than 300 active members. Grace Church is known for its strong education programs, mission outreach, musical offerings and arts focus.

(Right: Christ Church Christiana Hundred. See page 34.)

The Grand Opera House (above), center-city's most architecturally striking building, was constructed in 1871 under the auspices of the Masonic Order. Its distinctive cast-iron exterior, with Masonic symbol in the pediment above the doorway, and opulent Victorian interior were restored to their original glory in the mid-1970s. Today, the 1,190-seat Grand annually presents more than 400 performances a year in its main 1,190-seat theater and adjoining 300-seat "Baby Grand" theater. They range from symphony, dance and opera to stand-up comedy, jazz, world culture and programs for young people. Some rate it among the best venues in the country because of its acoustics and intimacy.

◄ Christ Church Christiana Hundred, the largest parish in the Episcopal Diocese of Delaware, was built in the mid-1850s to serve DuPont Company powder mill workers and owners alike. Financed by the company and members of the du Pont family, the Victorian Gothic Revival Style church sits on a hilltop adjacent to Hagley Museum, the site of the original du Pont black powder mills and family estate. Today, the church's 2,000-plus members continue a long tradition of outreach to the community, including various organizations and agencies that serve downtown Wilmington's population.

Wilmington's historic train station, one of the country's busiest, has been a city landmark since it was built in 1906 by the Pennsylvania Railroad. Designed in the Romanesque style by the noted Philadelphia firm of Furness, Evans and Company, the brick and terra cotta building was restored in 1984. Nearby, at the entrance to the Tubman-Garrett Riverfront Park on the Christina, a plaque set in a flower bed (below) recalls an important chapter in Wilmington's history. The 2.4-acre park is named in honor of abolitionist Harriet Tubman, renowned for her leadership role in the Underground Railroad, and Thomas Garrett, who provided refuge at his Quaker Hill home for slaves traveling from bondage to freedom.

Eleutherian Mills, the first du Pont family home in the United States, was built by Eleuthère Irénee du Pont in 1803. An avid botanist, du Pont created the French-style gardens that brighten the landscape in front of the home. It sits just uphill from the Brandywine River and the DuPont powder yards. To the left of the home is E. I. du Pont's original office, fully restored to the way it was in the 1850s when E.I.'s son Henry ran the business and lived in the house. Today the home, office and gardens are part of Hagley Museum and Library and included on public tours.

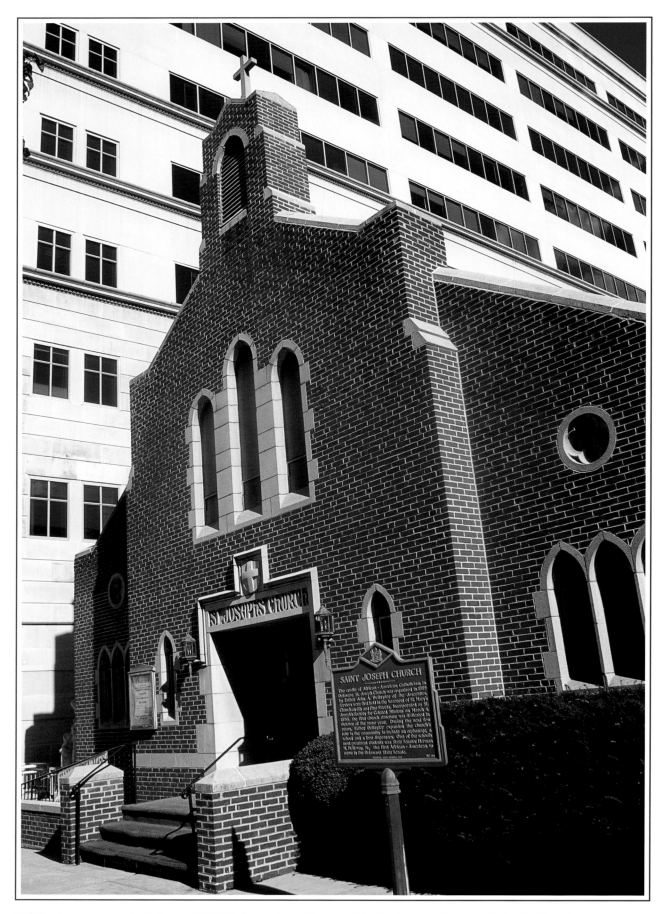

While the corporate buildings of MBNA have risen all around it, St. Joseph's Roman Catholic Church continues to thrive. The Franciscan Friars who minister to the 400 families that make up the dynamic community of faith give credit to MBNA for being a good and helpful neighbor. Originally established in 1889 to minister to the African-American residents of the city, it now has a diverse membership. The red brick church was built in 1948 to replace the original frame church edifice that was destroyed by fire in 1947. In its history, but no longer in existence, are the country's first orphanage for black males and a school run by Franciscan sisters.

Simple and dignified, this small church once served as a hospital and later gave up its site for a library. It was built in 1740 on 10th and Market Streets as Wilmington's first Presbyterian Church just after the city received its charter from King George II. Following the Battle of the Brandywine on September 2, 1777, the British used the church as a hospital. In 1916, it was moved to its present location at the foot of West Street overlooking the Brandywine River to make way for construction of the Wilmington Institute Free Library. Home of the Colonial Dames of America in Delaware, it is open to the public from 2 to 4 p.m. on the second Saturday of the month from April through October.

Nemours Mansion and Gardens, the former 300-acre estate of Alfred I. duPont, is named after the du Pont ancestral home in north central France. The formal French gardens, their design influenced by duPont's many trips to Europe, include a working carillon tower (right photo) and natural woodlands. The 1910 mansion, an excellent example of a modified Louis XVI French château, has 102 rooms furnished with fine period antiques, rare oriental rugs, tapestries and paintings dating back as far as the 15th century. It is closed for renovation until spring 2007 when tours will resume.

◀ The historic Wilmington & Brandywine Cemetery, established in 1843, spreads out over 24 acres on the west side of Wilmington, between northbound I-95 and the city skyline. Among the 20,500 people buried here are veterans of the Civil War and the War of 1812 and Dr. John McKinley of Ireland, the only known foreign-born governor of the state, in 1777. It continues as an active cemetery.

The Alfred I. duPont Hospital for Children, adjacent to Nemours, has served thousands from around the world since it was founded in 1940. Together, the hospital and the Nemours Children's Clinic, which provides services at several regional locations, are the academic partner of Thomas Jefferson University and Jefferson Medical College in Philadelphia.

Rain or shine, snow or squall, Admiral Samuel Francis du Pont greets visitors to Rockford Park at the Tower Road entrance. This statue of the Civil War hero stood in Du Pont Circle in Washington, D.C., from 1884 until 1920, when it was moved to Wilmington, du Pont's hometown. In the background, Rockford Tower, a distinctive and popular landmark, stands watch over Rockford Park, an expansive playground and meeting place located in the Highlands neighborhood. Noted sculptor Launt Thompson created the statue. At unveiling ceremonies in D.C. on December 20, 1884, U.S. Senator Thomas F. Bayard of Delaware was the principal speaker.

The young professionals who kick back at Kelly's Logan House in Trolley Square with a brew or bowl of chili carry on a tradition that goes back some 140 years. Originally named after a Civil War hero, General John Logan, the brick building has hosted such notable figures as Al Capone, Wild Bill Hickock and boxer John L. Sullivan. In the early 20th century, patrons came by trolley that ran up and down Delaware Avenue to the station across the street from the Logan House. Today's trendy Trolley Square bustles with approximately 80 galleries, shops, restaurants and professional service shops.

The oldest active firehouse in Delaware, Station 5 on Gilpin Avenue near 18th Street was organized in 1853 as the Water Witch Steam Company. In front of the 1893 firehouse, near Trolley Square, is its 1953 Mack fire engine, now used in parades only. The historic vehicle ties in with the Wilmington Fire Museum scheduled to be located on the second floor. Total personnel numbers 14 for Station 5, the second busiest in the city, making 1,440 runs last year.

From Rockford Tower, a panoramic view of Wilmington's skyline extending from the Chase Manhattan Centre south to the twin spans of the Delaware Memorial Bridge.

Places

If you stand in the middle of Rodney Square, the heart of downtown Wilmington, and slowly make a 180-degree turn, you'll glimpse high points in the city's history, both real and symbolic, and get a sense of its dynamic 21st century personality. Clustered here are institutions, corporations and, by association, individuals and ideas that have driven Wilmington forward for centuries.

The dramatic statue of Caesar Rodney astride his horse recalls a favorite Delaware story about the patriot's grueling over-night ride to Philadelphia in 1776 to cast a crucial vote for the country's independence. This highlighted a career that made him one of the state's most distinguished statesmen and the square's namesake. Across Market Street from the statue is DuPont's corporate headquarters, moved here in 1903 from the banks of the Brandywine where the company was founded a century earlier. Management had considered New York City, too, but Rodney Square won out. That decision launched Wilmington's transition from industrial town to modern corporate city. Long the state's largest private employer, DuPont was recently edged out by MBNA, the giant credit card bank. Its international headquarters face DuPont from across Rodney Square. MBNA's move to downtown Wilmington in 1995 brought new energy to the city.

With its grand classical architecture, the 1917 public building on the south side of Rodney Square could get by on its looks alone. The former courthouse provides a symbolic link to two state laws that have greatly influenced the city's economy. The 1899 Delaware Corporation Law, which made it easy for businesses to incorporate here, has resulted in 58 percent of the Fortune 500 companies doing just that. In 1981 the Financial Center Development Act gave credit-card banks the freedom to set interest rates and a big incentive to set up business here. More than 30 did, including MBNA, which now owns the public building as part of its large downtown campus.

The thriving educational and cultural dimensions of Wilmington are represented by the elegant Beaux Arts building that is the Wilmington Institute Free Library, opened in 1928. The DuPont Theatre in the world-class Hotel du Pont and the nearby Grand Opera House, active performing arts venues, star in the city's vibrant cultural life. From the upper levels of the Residences at Rodney Square, an upscale apartment building behind the library, city dwellers can look out over Rodney Square. These 275 apartments are among some 1,000 new housing units that have spurred a back-to-the-city trend. In minutes, these residents can be enjoying beautiful riverfront parks and the wide-open spaces of chateau country.

Wilmington Trust blended the new with the old in 1983 when it established its headquarters on the north side of the square. The 102-year-old institution built a modern office tower that rose from a 1930s federal building, effectively incorporating its richly ornamented façade.

If it's June when you're standing on the grass-covered square itself—once a reservoir—listen for the rousing DuPont Clifford Brown Jazz Festival; if it's Wednesday, pick up some tomatoes at the farmer's market. At holiday time, cheer a passing parade, join in the singing at Caroling on the Square or celebrate New Year's Eve at First Night. In the first five years of the 21st century, the city's revitalization has picked up, setting a spirited pace not seen for decades.

The Farmer's Market in Rodney Square, managed by Downtown Visions, an affiliate of the Wilmington Renaissance Corporation.

The hills come alive with the joy of spring blooms at Winterthur, an American Country Estate. Seasonal changes are particularly dramatic in the 60-acre naturalistic garden that is part of the property's 982 acres. Founder Henry Francis du Pont (1880-1969) selected choice plants from around the world to enhance the natural setting, arranging them in lyrical color combinations that bloom from late January to November.

A walker wends his way through one of Brandywine Park's many wooded paths, close enough to hear the Brandywine River rush by and just a few minutes from downtown. The 178-acre urban park stretches along a one-mile run of the river. Founded in 1885, it was added to the National Historic Register in 1976. One of four state parks in Wilmington, Brandywine attracts strollers, joggers, picnickers and naturalists. A Sensory Trail invites the visually impaired to enjoy the wonders of nature.

Spectacular geologic formations rise up from the paths of Alapocas Woods located along the Brandywine River west of the city. These formations, the result of the park being situated between the Piedmont and coastal plain zones, are unique in Delaware. The forested retreat connects to the Alapocas Run State Park and is part of the Delaware Greenways.

From the rooftop of Park Plaza condominiums, the view looking south over the city extends from one of Ursuline Academy's Gothic-style buildings and the Cool Springs Reservoir to elegant homes on 10th Street and beyond. When Cool Springs Reservoir was completed in 1877, another city reservoir occupied what is now Rodney Square.

Looking west from the Chase Manhattan Centre downtown toward St. Francis Hospital in Little Italy, the rooftops of the Mother AUFCMP Church on Franklin Street and Holy Trinity Greek Orthodox Church on Broom Street stand out amid the row homes and trees.

Elegant classical fountains, a curved bench and bright blooms merely hint at the widespread beauty of the formal Marian Coffin Gardens at Gibraltar, a former estate. The Italianate home that sits in the middle of the six-acre property was built in 1844 by John Rodney Brinkle, grandnephew of Delaware patriot Caesar Rodney. He and his family lived there until 1909 when philanthropist, preservationist and amateur horticulturist Hugh Rodney Sharp and his wife, Isabella du Pont Sharp, purchased the property. They hired Coffin to design the formal gardens. Originally completed in 1923, the gardens had long been neglected until the non-profit Preservation Delaware came to the rescue in the late 1990s, restoring them to their original grandeur and opening them to the public.

The Wilmington campus of Delaware Technical & Community College is one of four statewide that provide open admission at the associate degree level. The college's educational mix includes career, developmental and transfer education, lifelong learning, workforce education and training, and community services.

The Ships Tavern District is reborn as a successful residential-retail area. The city and Wilmington Renaissance Corp., a privately funded economic development group, orchestrated the $25 million redevelopment project of what had long been a rundown section of lower Market Street. The completed first phase: 22 historic buildings on the west side, rejuvenated and refurbished, with its Ships Tavern Mews comprising 86 apartments. Vassar Interiors (right), offering contemporary furniture, art and decorative accessories, was one of the first of several shops to open on the ground level with more to come. The district's name comes from the former Sign of the Ship Tavern that once operated at 230 N. Market St.

Further up Market Street, the holiday season arrives at the sleek residents' lounge in the grand lobby of the Residences at Rodney Square. Once the home of Delaware Trust, the building was converted by the Buccini/Pollin group to upscale apartments with views that look out over the Wilmington Library to Rodney Square.

Leave it to art students to come up with the most creative Halloween party costumes, as did Eric Walters of the Delaware College of Art and Design. His interpretation of a painting by the Surrealist artist Magritte earned him first place in a competition held at the college. DCAD served as a catalyst for downtown revitalization when it opened in 1997 in an Art Deco building that had once served as headquarters for a utilities company.

From a vantage point several stories up in the Hotel du Pont, a look down on the First & Central Presbyterian Church side of Rodney Square highlights the graphic designs on the streets. One of the Cool City Cars that was part of a public art project presented by Wilmington Renaissance Corporation elicits smiles of appreciation.

The Delaware Sports Museum and Hall of Fame at the Daniel Frawley Stadium on Wilmington's Riverfront celebrates 150 years of the state's sports history. Recent headline-grabbing feats, such as the state's first Little League World Series team, are touted in special exhibitions that heighten the appeal of the museum's well-designed permanent displays. Memorabilia, artifacts, uniforms and photographs cover everything from Judy Johnson, the city's Negro League hero and National Baseball Hall of Famer, to Olympians and high school and college teams.

Renowned marine artist Wyland used this office-building façade on Martin Luther King Boulevard as the canvas for one of his marine-themed murals known as "whaling walls." Completed in 1993, it is one of 90-plus throughout the country. For passers-by, the public art is a constant reminder of Wilmington's proximity to the sea. Built in the late 19th century, the unnamed building once housed a carriage manufacturing company and later, a theater. Today, it is home to various business tenants. Its owners are exploring ways to restore the weather-worn mural.

David Bromberg & Associates, Fine Violins, which set up shop in 2002 in a 19th century building on Market Street Mall, trades in rare instruments and produces bows and violins. Bromberg's shop boasts the largest collection of antique American-made violins in the country, numbering some 200. A nationally known performing musician, Bromberg has become the world's preeminent expert on American violin makers. Two master craftsmen on his staff create some of the finest instruments made in the United States today. Working in cooperation with city officials, Bromberg and his wife, sculptor Nancy Josephson, who live on the upper levels of the four-story building, have committed to being cultural ambassadors for Wilmington.

The University of Delaware's Academy of Lifelong Learning thrives at Arsht Hall on the university's Wilmington campus. Here, some 1,200 people age 50 and over pursue intellectual development and cultural stimulation through classes that range from art history and Shakespeare to chemistry fundamentals and T'ai Chi. Seminars, socials, concerts, art exhibitions and travel programs enhance the program. The Academy has earned a national reputation as a leader, often a model, of college and university efforts to reach out to adults of retirement age.

More than 9,000 commuter students attend Wilmington College, a private, non-sectarian school that offers undergraduate- and graduate-level degree programs in a variety of career areas. Its main campus (in photo) is in New Castle with other locations in Dover, Georgetown and Rehoboth Beach.

On one corner of Rodney Square, and extending to several adjacent buildings, stands the international headquarters for MBNA, the world's largest independent credit card issuer. The Bracebridge building, designed to reflect the square's traditional and neoclassical elements, opened in 1995. With 10,500 employees in Delaware, it is the state's largest private employer. The company has grown steadily since it first opened in 1982 in a former supermarket in Ogletown, boosting the local economy and generously supporting various community organizations. MBNA was one of the first of 30-plus companies to take advantage of the 1981 Financial Center Development Act legislation that gave credit card banks the freedom to set interest rates.

The morning sun brightens the façades of the Chase Manhattan Centre office tower (rear) and Hercules Plaza, opened in 1988 and 1983, respectively, and viewed from the Market Street Bridge. The prominent architectural firm Skidmore, Owings & Merrill of Chicago designed the Chase Manhattan Centre. Hercules' modern granite-and-glass building, corporate headquarters for the global manufacturer of specialty chemicals, was the centerpiece of the Brandywine Gateway development of the 1980s. Kinetic Sculptures by Ken Davis, one of Wilmington's many works of public art, adorns Hercules Plaza. Three large marble spheres—one weighs three tons—spin atop marble bases, their movement powered by water flowing up through the bases.

In the midst of a wooded landscape, DuPont's Experimental Station Laboratory spreads out over 152 acres. The site sits across the Brandywine River from where E.I. du Pont founded the company and a few miles from corporate headquarters in downtown Wilmington. Some 2,000 employees work here in 48 buildings with a site infrastructure capable of supporting a city of 6,000-8,000 homes. High-achieving scientists who've donned lab coats here include a winner of the Nobel Prize in Chemistry, the inventor of Kevlar and several who pioneered the development of polymers such as nylon, neoprene rubber and environmentally friendly herbicides.

◀ South Bancroft Parkway curves its way through the Union Park Gardens neighborhood, built on the site of an old ballpark. Its family-friendly atmosphere and well-landscaped and maintained homes that are reasonably priced make it a magnet for firefighters and police officers. Its thriving neighborhood association, with events for young and old, contribute to its reputation as a "hot" neighborhood in real estate circles.

Wilmington Friends School, the oldest school in Delaware, was founded by local Quakers in 1748 to educate children of diverse backgrounds. The co-educational day school serves more than 800 students in grades pre-kindergarten through 12. The school established Delaware's first kindergarten and kindergarten teacher-training program. Wilmington Friends was among the first schools in the nation to host students from other countries, through the American Field Service.

Spring goes over the top in Brandywine Park, where the flowering trees beg to be photographed or painted. In 1930, J. Ernest Smith donated the weeping cherry trees to the city, fulfilling a wish of his wife, Josephine Tatnall Smith, who, unfortunately, died before seeing the trees in bloom. He dedicated the fountain to his wife in 1933. It incorporates the romantic tastes of 16th-century Italy for the beautiful (cherubs and flowers) and the grotesque (lions, rams and masks). Lines from the poem *Wordsworth* by John Greenleaf Whittier are engraved on the base of the fountain.

◄ Today it's the P.S. du Pont Elementary School. When it opened in 1935, it was the largest high school in Delaware and was named in honor of Pierre S. du Pont for the millions of dollars he had spent and the extensive time he devoted to improving education throughout the state.

At the Brandywine Zoo, located on 13 landscaped acres in Brandywine Park just a few minutes from center city, visitors chuckle at the playful river otters dashing around and marvel at the exotic Siberian tigers whose mere presence commands attention. The two male-female pairs share the well-designed space with some 150 other animals, reptiles and birds as the zoo celebrates its centennial anniversary. The Siberian tigers, Ashley and Sergei, represent their extinct species with dignity. Meanwhile, the river otters play out a sad love story, at least for the male, Jester. He's been pursuing Delta for about five years, but she's simply not interested. Caw and Max, the two colorful macaws, practice good PR, sometimes calling out "Hello" when a visitor walks by.

On November 21, 1963, President John F. Kennedy cut the ribbon officially opening I-95 in one of his last official acts before he was assassinated. Looking north (right), beyond the street overpasses, the Park Plaza condomium building rises just before the highway crosses the Brandywine River. The new AAA building (above, center) and the Residences at Christina Landing across the Christina River headline construction projects on the burgeoning Wilmington Riverfront. Now one of the nation's busiest corridors, I-95 facilitates travel and helps boost economic growth. But when it was first built in the early '60s, the project caused pain for the residents and businesses it displaced.

Rockford Park boasts large open spaces surrounded by wooded areas, making it ideal for picnics, jogging, flying kites and playing ball. Whatever the season, the historic Rockford Tower stands out as the park's centerpiece. Built between 1899 and 1902, the 115-foot-tall, natural-fieldstone tower is an example of the Italian Renaissance Revival style, an esthetic treasure with a half-million-gallon tank that supplies water to city residents.

The trees around Hoopes Reservoir flaunt their fall beauty. The 200-acre reservoir, completed in 1933, stores two billion gallons of water that assure emergency back-up for all of northern Delaware. Spring-fed and 130 feet at its deepest point, the reservoir stands on property once owned by T. Coleman du Pont. No fishing, boating or swimming are allowed in the 50-degree water.

Bellevue State Park's lavish spread of fall colors is caught in a double-your-pleasure moment. Enhanced recreation opportunities at the 328-acre public park include trails for walking, jogging and cycling; a 1-1/8-mile fitness track that circles a catch-and-release fishing pond stocked with bass, catfish, and sunfish; tennis facilities with outdoor clay courts; a modern equestrian facility; and picnic pavilions. The park's historic Bellevue Hall mansion was transformed by William H. du Pont, Jr., from a Gothic Revival castle into a replica of President James Madison's home, Montpelier. Now a site for meetings, receptions and weddings, the mansion commands a grand view of the estate.

Colorful banners on the Rodney Square side of the DuPont Building promote the DuPont Theatre, which has presented a Broadway series since 1913, plus other entertainment and children's programs. The 1,251-seat theater also hosts business meetings and private parties.

Delaware Theatre Company, the area's only resident professional theatre, was among the first to move to the now-booming Riverfront Wilmington when it built its theater there in 1985. Founded in 1978, the theater's annual season of plays includes a mix of the classics as well as contemporary and new works. It brings noted professional actors, directors and designers to Wilmington from New York and beyond.

A traveling exhibition, one of more than 30 presented annually by the Delaware Center for the Contemporary Arts, is shown in one of its seven galleries. One of the country's leading contemporary art spaces, the non-collecting museum, which has become an arts and entertainment drawing card for Riverfront Wilmington, recently marked its 25th anniversary. Artists covet the 26 on-site studios housed here, and a variety of community organizations use its auditorium and attractive space for meetings and events.

The exhibition *Sacred Memory: Picture Painters and Relic Makers from the South* at DCCA focused on work by southern artists with little or no formal art training or influence from the contemporary art world. Often called outsider or visionary artists, these individuals and their artwork provide a highly personal sense of passion and honesty, and they captivate the imaginations of viewers while providing insight to another world. Shown is the work of William Thomas Thompson of South Carolina (left) and an expansive mural by James Buddy Snipes (above) of Alabama.

An historic mural saluting 25 leaders in the Wilmington African American community covers the 10th Street side of the Pine Street rowhouse where environmental activist Hazel Brown lives. A member of the Delaware Center for Horticulture's board, Brown is among those in the mural. Dutch Burton, active in desegregating restaurants, is prominently portrayed in the circle at left. The garden, which honors the late Hattie M. Phelan, is part of the Community Gardens program sponsored by the Center for Horticulture.

Art and nature combine for a striking effect at Valley Garden on property owned by Community Housing Inc. at 8th and Jefferson Streets. The dramatic mural by Roldan Weist illustrates the riots that broke out in Wilmington streets in the late '60s following the assassination of Martin Luther King, Jr. The snow-covered beds will bloom in the spring, a testament to the Delaware Center for Horticulture's Community Gardens program.

The Delaware Art Museum's major expansion, in process when photographed from its north side, includes greatly increased gallery space (left) to present its world-renowned collections of American art and English Pre-Raphaelite art, as well as traveling exhibitions. One of the area's most important cultural assets, the museum's newly expanded facility includes an education wing with studios (right) and the state's first sculpture park for exhibitions of commissioned and loaned sculpture by nationally renowned artists. The nine-acre sculpture park is located along Delaware Greenways, bridging parkland and the Kentmere Parkway residential area that surrounds the museum.

For decades, Wilmingtonians have enjoyed the sight of rowers in their shells gliding on the
Christina. The changing skyline brings new sights almost every day.

The Rivers

The rivers that wrap around Wilmington have been on a power trip for centuries. They provided food and transportation for the original residents, the Lenni Lenape Indians. They brought European settlers here, powered mills and steel industries, moved goods in and out and continue to attract people to live and play along their banks.

In 1638, the city's first European settlers sailed up the Delaware River and the broad and navigable Christina to what is now the 7th Street Peninsula. They were Swedes who named the river in honor of their queen.

In the 18th century, Quakers used the Brandywine River's energy to turn waterwheels that helped flour mills flourish near the present-day Market Street Bridge. The prized "Brandywine Superfine" flour brought by sailing ships to the West Indies and Europe garnered international fame for Wilmington. Joshua and Thomas Gilpin built a paper mill on the Brandywine in 1787. Another entrepreneur, Eleuthère Irénée du Pont of France, launched the international giant DuPont in 1802 when he established his gunpowder manufacturing company upstream on the Brandywine. Joseph Bancroft's cotton mill joined the ranks in 1831 and became one of Delaware's biggest and most important companies.

Shipbuilding prospered on the Christina River from the late 19th century into the mid-20th century. Harlan & Hollingsworth and Pusey & Jones made Wilmington the largest producer of iron vessels in the country. The latter firm's first contract was for a Civil War sloop. During World War I the company employed 2,000. During World War II, more than 10,000 people were employed building ships and military landing craft that helped win the war.

Residents would gather on the riverfront to celebrate ship launchings, with special interest in the grand luxury yachts destined for the America's Cup races. Some brought national attention to the local shipbuilding companies and generated hometown pride during the races.

In 1923, the Port of Wilmington opened at the confluence of the Christina and Delaware Rivers. Designed to support the growing shipbuilding, railroad car construction and carriage-making industries along the Christina, the port's tonnage that year was 17,000 tons. Today, its annual import-export cargo tonnage tops a whopping 5 million tons.

During the post-war decades, the Christina riverfront was largely neglected, while along the Brandywine, the oasis of parks first established in 1885 continued to blossom. Revitalization of the Christina riverfront started slowly at the end of the 20th century, but soon it was moving full-speed ahead, driven by the Riverfront Development Corporation, a public-private venture. Major development that continues today has transformed the riverfront into a thriving center of business, culture and entertainment. Restored industrial buildings include a conference center and an art museum. Newly constructed outlet shops are linked to a number of restaurants, a marketplace and a theater by a beautifully landscaped 1.5-mile river walk that honors the river's past with a series of plaques recognizing historic highlights. Four Gantry cranes that were used to launch ships dot the river walk, the highest-profile reminders of the area's industrial past. And the $125 million Residences at Christina Landing, a complex of townhouses and apartment tower and the area's first residential development, is rising on the riverfront.

As the 21st century settles in, Wilmington's rivers aren't settling for going with the flow, they're directing it. Their power trip continues.

The Tubman-Garrett Riverfront Park honors abolitionists Harriet Tubman and Quaker Thomas Garrett, both leaders in the Underground Railroad movement.

Smith's Bridge spreads distinctively across the Brandywine River in a woodsy spot north of Winterthur and close to the Pennsylvania state line, a 2002 version of its original self. First built in 1839, the 145-foot bridge was destroyed by arson in 1961. It is one of only two covered bridges in Delaware.

It looks like a 19th century scene, but it's totally 21st century. And not a movie setting either. Elegant antique carriages carry riders in period dress along the Brandywine River on the weekend of Winterthur's Point to Point races, the premier see-and-be-seen event during the month of May.

The charms of Breck's Mill and its woodsy setting (above) are mirrored in the Brandywine where its waters pause for a placid moment before rushing over the waterfall ahead. In the 19th century, cotton and woolen goods were made at the mill, preserved as part of Hagley Museum. It has been restored into stylish space for two art galleries where visitors enjoy expansive views of the river along with the works of art.

The corporate giant DuPont started here in 1802 when Eleuthère Irénee du Pont decided it was an ideal spot to plant his gunpowder works using the power of the Brandywine River to make it grow. In the foreground is Henry Clay Mill, originally a cotton-spinning factory dating back to 1814. Today it is where Hagley Museum presents exhibitions and greets visitors for tours that include restored mills, a workers' community and the ancestral home and gardens of the du Pont family.

Walker's Mill (above), powered by the rapids of the Brandywine, produced textiles from 1815 to the late 1930s. Just downstream from Hagley Museum, the mill is owned by the DuPont Company on grounds that spread out over 235 acres.

The gracefully arched B&O railroad bridge and the Augustine Cutoff vehicular bridge loom over the swinging bridge that crosses the Brandywine. But only on the swinging bridge can travelers—in this case walkers and runners—stop and contemplate the river running under them. And only on the swinging bridge do users get to experience the reason for its name—it moves a little when you walk on it. Long a favorite of photographers, the swinging bridge dates back to the early 20th century when it served as a convenient crossing for folks going to the paper mills on the north side of the Brandywine.

Anglers try out their luck in the Brandywine with the Washington Street Bridge, the Hercules building and Chase Manhattan Centre as backdrop.

To enjoy the Brandywine slowly and sweetly, nothing beats tubing along the river's surface with plenty of time to savor the leafy trees along its banks, the sun sparkling on the water and the birds twittering overhead.

While the Christina River isn't straight and wide, it offers the calm waters that rowers seek—about 10 miles worth. Rowing out of their riverfront boathouse, members of The Wilmington Rowing Center prepare for action (above) and glide along the Christina River with the city skyline as a backdrop. Some of the club's 150 members, who range in age from 13 to 73, compete in regattas and other races. The club offers learn-to-row programs and annually hosts the Diamond State Regatta, considered one of the premier events of its type in the country.

Riders on the Wilmington Trolley can experience a history moment when they hop on the rubber-tired vehicle designed to recall turn-of-the-century streetcar transportation. For a mere 25 cents, it offers service between Rodney Square and the Wilmington Riverfront with frequent stops along the way. The trolley's rounds begin and end in front of the Bank One Center on the Riverfront, a regional convention/conference facility with 85,000 square feet of meeting, banquet and exhibit space.

One of the city's largest family events, DuPont RiverFest draws up to 10,000 to the Wilmington Riverfront in September for fun and games, food and music. The festivities stretch along the Christina's Riverwalk from Kahunaville to the Train Station, where the Delaware Transportation Festival adds to the fun. Proceeds benefit the Boys and Girls Clubs.

The pace of development along the Christina River marches steadily forward. Scheduled for 2005 completion are the AAA Mid-Atlantic building (above, foreground), a Commonwealth Group project, and the Christina Landing luxury residential community with high-rise apartments (above and left), a Buccini/Pollen project. Viewed from another angle (left), the established commercial real estate just a block from the river includes the Christina Gateway and its Bank One building.

Delaware's Tall Ship, the Kalmar Nyckel, serves as the state's goodwill ambassador at festivals and a host of other events up and down the East Coast, from Virginia to Massachusetts. Built by volunteers in the 1990s, the modern-day beauty is a replica of the ship that in 1638 brought Wilmington's first settlers from Sweden and Finland. When it's at home in Wilmington, the Kalmar Nyckel offers sailing and education opportunities. Party planners like it as a venue for events, whether it's docked or for excursions and adventure sails. Owned and operated by a non-profit foundation, the eight-sail ship is frequently used as a catalyst for tourism and economic development. EDIS headquarters (above) serve as a backdrop as it moves along the Christina. Using wind power (right) it sails on the Christina toward the Delaware River.

The University of Delaware Women's Crew, which rows out of the WYRA Boathouse on the Christina River, gets to work on a cloudy day. The men's crew from U of D and the Wilmington Youth Rowing program share the boathouse.

◀ The Brandywine River goes with the flow under the Washington Street Memorial Bridge headed toward its confluence with the Christina River. Alfred I. du Pont chaired the commission that oversaw the building of the bridge in the early 1920s. One of the bridge's pylons lists the names of Delawareans who died while serving in World War I.

The super-size bustle of daily activity at the Port of Wilmington—gigantic cranes moving massive loads from and onto ships from all over the world—reflects its importance to the city's economy. Located at the confluence of the Christina and Delaware Rivers, 65 miles from the Atlantic Ocean, the port ranks number one in the country for its imports of fresh fruit and is the world's largest banana port. Because of its strategic location and state-of-the-art facilities, the port has attracted some of the world's top produce shippers, led by Dole Fresh Fruit Company and Chiquita Fresh North American. They come into Wilmington every week, year-round, with fruit to supply more than a third of the nation's population, transported by businesses like Murphy Marine Services (above right). But there's a lot more than grapes and apples coming through the port. It's a major distribution hub for Australian and New Zealand beef, and a key Mid-Atlantic auto-port for imports of Volkswagens and Audis and for exports of General Motors and other autos. Its annual import-export cargo volume totals a whopping 5 million tons.

At the southern end of the multimillion-dollar project that has created economic vitality along the Christina River is a environmental endeavor that honors a former governor, the Russell W. Peterson Urban Wildlife Refuge. The Riverfront Development Corporation, which has overseen the entire development project, has cleaned up more than 300 acres of the riverfront land since 1995.

◄ The Brandywine River and the ice-laden, tidal Christina River flirt with one another at the approach to the Seventh Street Peninsula. Delaware's Tall Ship is moored in the Christina near its home base, the Kalmar Nyckel Shipyard, where its construction and launching took place and where crew training continues. Visitors to the shipyard, adjacent to the original Kalmar Nyckel's landing site, get a taste of the ancient art of ship making and the colonial history of Delaware.

Recalling the days when the Christina River bustled with ship-building activity, one of the four brightly painted Gantry cranes used to launch ships now adds a point of historic interest along Wilmington's Riverwalk. With an eye to the future, the statue of Gov. Russell W. Peterson is positioned to look south where the eponymous Urban Wildlife Refuge moves forward on acres of marshland.

The Riverfront Market in a restored historic warehouse attracts huge lunch-time crowds for its sushi, Thai cuisine, deli sandwiches and rotisserie specialties. Riverfront Produce, which adds freshly squeezed juices and fresh salsas to its bountiful mix of fruits and vegetables, attracts customers from throughout the region as well as those who work nearby.

One of the many charms of Wilmington's revitalized Riverfront is its 1.3-mile pedestrian Riverwalk, beautifully landscaped and well lighted. It runs along the Christina River and curbside to the lively Riverfront Market, several restaurants, two museums, a theatre and businesses in recycled industrial buildings. Attractive plaques along the way provide snippets of information about the area's historic roots. ▶

People

A delicious taste of Wilmington: Crowds gather for the Vendemmia da Vinci wine festival at Tubman-Garrett Park with the steadily expanding skyline as backdrop and the Kalmar Nyckel tall ship adding an historic note.

The People

The city that used to sleep from 5 to 9, calling it a day after the lawyers, bankers and chemists went home to the suburbs, is changing its ways. For years Wilmington's population of 72,000 has ballooned to about double that number when open-for-business signs were posted. During the rest of the week, you could roll the proverbial bowling ball down Market Street. Now, for the first time in decades, people are moving into the city. Lots of people. And they're helping change the dynamics of center city and the Christina riverfront.

More than 1,000 new residential units—loft apartments, stylish condos and riverfront homes—have opened or are under construction and selling well. Their occupants can walk to the new restaurants, to entertainment venues and to special events, all increasing in number and variety. Concurrently, more downtown workers stay in town and more suburbanites come into town and the riverfront to join in the fun. The Grand Opera House alone, for example, presents 100-plus performances a year, from symphony, dance and opera to stand-up comedy, jazz, world culture and programs for young people. Theatre N, the first downtown movie theater in decades, shows art and independent films every weekend. Riverfront pioneer Delaware Theatre Company offers an adventurous mix of contemporary and classic plays, and the nearby Delaware Center for Contemporary Art mounts equally adventurous exhibitions, about 30 every year. The Delaware Art Museum, the state's premier fine arts institution, is poised to significantly raise the city's cultural profile with its expanded facility and new sculpture park near Rockford Park.

Wilmingtonians turn out by the thousands to wave their ethnic flags at a host of high-spirited festivals and events. They soak up and eat up Old Country flavor at the week-long Italian Festival, the tasty Greek Festival, the colorful Hispanic Day Parade and the Polish-proud Pulaski Day parade. When it's St. Patrick's turn to be saluted with a parade, everybody's Irish. The elegant St. Lucia Festival in Old Swedes Church honors the city's deep Swedish roots that go back to the 17th century. City residents rise and shine for the spirited August Quarterly, and they schmooze with the horsey set at the quintessential people-watching event, Winterthur's Point to Point. Music lovers groove at the major DuPont Clifford Brown Jazz Festival in Rodney Square, and on the riverfront, at the Bob Marley Festival, the Blues Festival and Shipyard Concerts. They cool off with a cone at the Ice Cream Festival at Rockwood Mansion Park, with some Victoriana mixed in, and rev their engines at the Hagley Car Show. Some 20,000 welcome fall and indulge their shopping urges at the Brandywine Arts Festival which spreads out along the Brandywine River. DuPont RiverFest draws up to 10,000 to the Wilmington Riverfront for fun and games, food and music.

Northern Delaware boasts two high seasons for enjoying simple outdoor pleasures. The weather gods bless spring and fall with extended periods of moderate temperatures enhanced by an abundance of natural beauty, such as the glorious cherry blossoms in Brandywine Park and fall foliage that rivals Vermont's. Residents head to nearby parks and chateau country to walk, run, play softball and tennis, fly kites, spread out a picnic or visit a Siberian tiger at the Brandywine Zoo. On the calm Christina River, crews quietly oar their sleek boats while nearby, baseball fans cheer the Wilmington Blue Rocks at Frawley Stadium. Sledders and cross-country skiers usually find enough snow to get a winter-sports fix or two. Wilmington is a city for all seasons and many tastes, and it's growing more so day by day, and evening by evening.

Hot sounds at the DuPont Clifford Brown Jazz Festival.

Faith and begorra! The 30th annual St. Patrick's Day parade along King Street basked in springtime sunshine and big crowds that reached as many as 10,000, according to some estimates. They enjoyed adorable Irish dancers, pipe bands, two fife and drum bands, St. Patrick and lots of wearin' o' the the green. Above right: Two members of the sponsoring Irish Club of Delaware get into the spirit at the urging of a string band leader.

In the 34th annual Caesar Rodney Half Marathon, Delaware's oldest and preeminent footrace, the competitors ran on a typically cold and windy March day. Beginning and ending in Rodney square, the route included South Park Drive along the Brandywine.

Point to Point, presented by Winterthur, An American Country Estate, has reigned as the quintessential people-watching event for more than 25 years. It attracts more than 16,000 people on the first Sunday of May to the estate's rolling countryside. Steeplechase races anchor a full day of activities that range from fun to fancy—stick horse races for the kids, canine capers for the dogs and the traditional Antique Carriage Parade for everyone who appreciates the beauty of the surreys, wagons, carriages and their handsomely dressed riders.

The City Parks and Recreation Department serves up tennis lessons to 125 kids age eight to 14 in the Rodney Street Tennis Program held every summer. Certified tennis pro Harold Washington, of Glassboro, N.J., applies techniques that motivate the players to improve their game. Kids who play on the advanced level participate in area tournaments organized by the U.S. Tennis Association.

The LPGA Urban Youth Golf Program celebrates its 10th year of "helping to keep kids out of the rough." In 2004, more than 2,000 children were served, learning life skills such as integrity and leadership as well as how to hit the ball. The presenters give college scholarship help to every graduating senior who has been a participant, and they've been involved in installing several indoor and outdoor putting greens in Wilmington.

A skateboarder shows off the fun of his sport at a Wilmington Skate Project event held at Frawley Stadium.
He's helping raise funds for the non-profit's in-the-works skateboard park at Maryland Avenue and Linden Streets
under the I-95 overpass. Two or three of these events are held annually, says the project's leader, Kevin Kelly,
a Wilmington city councilman.

An easel painter who's a student of Wilmington artist Ed Loper uses the cast iron and glass conservatory that is part of the Victorian Rockwood Mansion for inspiration.

The Procession of Saints, a colorful parade of floats bearing statues of saints through the streets of Little Italy, wraps up the biggest ethnic celebration of them all, St. Anthony's Italian Festival. More than 250,000 enjoy the week-long celebration of everything Italian that ranks among the top 50 community events on the East Coast. For 30 years, St. Anthony of Padua Parish has hosted the lively event, serving up porkette sandwiches, spezzato (a tasty veal stew) and hundreds of pounds of spaghetti to keep energy levels high for the schmoozing, card-playing, carnival rides and cultural entertainment. Concerts in the church attract those looking for a quieter taste of the performing arts; traditional dance performances and instruction in the Tarantella Tent (right) inspired many spectators to perform themselves.

Traditional old-country dances—think Zorba the Greek—mix with the delights of spanokopita, baklava and other Greek treats at the annual Greek Festival, held in early June on the grounds of Holy Trinity Greek Orthodox Church.

The baseball gods were shining on the Wilmington Blue Rocks when they became an affiliate of the Boston Red Sox during the after-glow of their 2004 World Series Championship. The Blue Rocks team built up an enviable reputation and record of its own during its 11 years as the Class A affiliate of the Kansas City Royals, but now they get to bask in the glow of the Red Sox long-awaited-for achievement. The Blue Rocks play at Frawley Stadium on the Riverfront. On the Fourth of July, star-studded uniforms add style to sport. At every game, Rocky Bullwinkle, a popular team mascot, engages children in games, songs and lots of slapstick.

Every evening for one high-energy week in June, the annual DuPont Clifford Brown Jazz Festival draws fans to Rodney Square in the heart of downtown Wilmington and to nearby Willingtown Square (above right). The largest of its kind on the East Coast, the festival featured major jazz artists like drummer T.S. Monk, pianist Ahmad Jamal, and violinist Regina Carter, who performed with the Delaware Symphony. Singer Cassandra Wilson and the Jazz at Lincoln Center's Afro-Latin Jazz Orchestra closed out the eclectic festival on Sunday night at Winterthur, An American Country Estate, north of the city. Despite some downpours, more than 40,000 jazz fans took in the concerts.

◀ The DuPont Clifford Brown Jazz Festival entices people to stop for the music at Rodney Square.

The Taste of Wilmington family food festival attracts 5,000 hungry people to Frawley Stadium on the Wilmington Riverfront for samples of tasty food offered by restaurants and caterers, cooking demos and entertainment. Sponsored by 99.5-WJBR-FM, the event benefits the Food Bank of Delaware.

The treats are cool and so is the Victorian flavor at the annual Rockwood Ice Cream Festival held in Rockwood Mansion Park, owned by New Castle County. With Rockwood Museum, a Gothic Revival mansion, as the inspiration, volunteers create living history moments for the 70,000-plus visitors during the two-day event. Some re-enact Civil War moments; others teach how to make lace or bandboxes—from scratch, of course. Signora Bella juggles and walks a tightrope. Music, lawn games and fireworks add to the fun.

Fans of the Delaware Smash, World TeamTennis 2003 League Champions, cheer the hometown team at its new venue, the AstraZeneca Tennis Facility next to the Ronald McDonald House on Rockland Road. Crowds of more than 2000 showed up for the fast-paced matches with heightened buzz when Monica Seles competed. The former No. 1 women's tennis player in the world played as part of WTT's New York Sportimes team. AstraZeneca is presenting sponsor of the Smash.

With the Christina River as a backdrop, the Roots/Rockabilly Music Festival (left) and Shipyard Summer Concert Series bring an eclectic mix of music to appreciative fans. The Shipyard Concerts, on stage in July and August at Wilmington Riverfront's Dravo Plaza, serve up everything from country and rock 'n' roll to big band sounds.

Uplifting gospel music moves the receptive crowd at the August Quarterly, the nation's oldest African-American folk festival and religious celebration, dating back to slavery. A family-friendly spirit prevails throughout the weekend-long celebration, much of it at Tubman-Garrett Riverfront Park. A photography exhibit by the Historical Society of Delaware, worship services at the Mother African Union FCMP Church and a fashion show at Pharos Restaurant headline a full schedule of events.

◀ The Hot Rod Hoedown and Roots/Rockabilly Music Festival rocks the Riverfront on a sunny September Saturday. The music festival takes over Kahunaville; the car show reigns in its parking lot. On tap: custom, classic and specialty cars, and some hot rods, too.

Fans of rhythmic reggae got their fix at The People's Festival Tribute to Bob Marley in August at Tubman-Garrett Riverfront Park. About 5,000 attended the festival's 10th anniversary celebration.

Almost 7,000 blues fans were drawn to Tubman-Garrett Park on the Christina River to hear headliners Bo Diddley and Bobby Rush and other performers get together and jam at the Riverfront Blues Festival in August.

For long-time residents, fall doesn't officially begin until the Brandywine Arts Festival rolls out its bevy of tents along the banks of the Brandywine. About 20,000 come to see what the 250-plus artists and artisans from more than 30 states are showing and selling. They find cutting-edge clothing and jewelry, sculpture, painting and photography, plus refrigerator magnets, scented candles and dried-flower wreaths.

◄ The more than 500 antique cars and trucks at Hagley Museum's 9th annual Car Show give visitors the opportunity to drive through America's automotive history.

The feasts and festivities of Hispanic Heritage Month in September reach their colorful peak at the Hispanic Day Parade. Thousands come to cheer the floats, school bands, cultural groups, dancers and the grand marshal. Maria Matos, executive director of the Latin-American Community Center, has worn the crown, sharing the position of honor with the parade's Godmother and Godfather, a tribute to the culture's family focus.

Polish pride was on parade for the 63rd annual celebration honoring Revolutionary War hero Casimir Pulaski. Every October, Polish Heritage Month, high school bands and string bands march through the streets of the Hedgeville-Browntown section of town for the Pulaski Day parade, sponsored by the Delaware Division of the Polish-American Congress. To honor the 100th anniversary of St. Hedwig's Catholic church, a group of students from the church school sang Sto Lat, which means "May you live 100 years."

The Delaware State Police Pipes & Drums Corps add a classy touch to the St. Patrick's Day parade. Formed in December 2001, the group of 14 performs at police funerals and special events and some charity functions.

"A Revolutionary Afternoon in Brandywine Village" recalled a long-forgotten piece of American Revolutionary history— the contributions of free black soldiers and slaves who fought in the war. Brandywine Village was one of several stops during the reenactment which traced the original route the allied Revolutionary War soldiers followed, from Claymont downhill to the Wilmington Riverfront. In the elegant stone houses where patriotic Quaker millers lived, officers were lodged and their provisions replenished.

Mountain bikers take in the autumn-tinged beauty of the rolling countryside of Chateau Country, which never ceases to appeal, no matter the season.

A runner and his dog head up through Rockford Park toward its distinctive landmark, Rockford Tower, built at the highest point in the city, 330 feet above sea level.

Our enduring love affair with everything Italian, especially wine, food and song, drew more than a thousand people to Tubman-Garrett Riverfront Park for Wilmington's First Annual Vendemmia da Vinci. Beautiful fall weather blessed the high-spirited wine festival, organized by the Societa da Vinci, whose Italian-American members promote their cultural heritage. Officials from La Spezia, Italy, who have a formal trade agreement with New Castle County, added an Old Country touch by providing wine and cheese from their region. Salud!

Golfers at the Rock Manor Golf Club, a public golf course built in 1938 and just minutes from downtown Wilmington, bask in autumn's brilliant colors. The adjoining Blue Ball Project, which is transforming the area's roadways and natural areas into a gateway to the Brandywine Hundred communities, has provided for the expansion of the golf course to "championship length" or approximately 6,200 yards.

The Fieldstone Golf Club in Greenville, a private club about 10 minutes from downtown Wilmington, covers 185 acres of the rolling Piedmont hills typical of northern Delaware. It boasts dramatic elevation changes, bent-grass fairways and classic bunkering with a clubhouse set immediately over the 18th green.

Thousands of bundled-up parade lovers lined downtown Wilmington streets for the 42nd annual Wilmington Jaycees Christmas Parade on the day after Thanksgiving. Public officials waved from shiny antique cars. Scooby-Doo and Sponge Bob Square Pants pranced around on colorful floats. High school marching bands, baton twirlers and step dancers picked up the pace. Passing by the DuPont Playhouse entrance in the Hotel du Pont are the New Castle County Mounted Police (above) and the Delaware Technical and Community College float (right). Santa cheered the crowds as he wrapped up the hoopla, waving from the last float.

When the first snow of the season covers
the gentle slopes of Rockford Park, sleds,
toboggans and skis come out of storage
and giggles and whoops of joy resound
throughout the park.

Year after year at holiday time, the lights shine brightly on the trees at Rockwood Mansion Park, a New Castle County property, and an enormous red bow exuberantly wraps the Cherishables shop in Trolley Square.

Some 30,000 gathered in and around Rodney Square for First Night Wilmington, a family-friendly, New Year's Eve party. Celebrants enjoyed an artistic mix of performances by Philadelphia singer-songwriter Lauren Hart, continuous short films at Theatre N and art exhibits in the Community Services Building galleries. Young ice skaters showed off their stuff on a synthetic rink installed in front of the DuPont Theater at the Hotel du Pont. Fireworks topped off the fun, brightening the Caesar Rodney statue (right) and the Grand Opera House (above).

The elegant pageantry of the St. Lucia Festival lights up Old Swedes Episcopal Church. Taylor Long of Wilmington, wearing a crown of lighted candles, re-creates the role of St. Lucia in the traditional Swedish celebration of the winter solstice and Christmas.

Partners in Progress

The City of Wilmington

Founded in 1731, Wilmington was a city long before America was a nation.

Centuries before European settlers arrived, the land at the confluence of the Christina, Brandywine and Delaware Rivers provided a hospitable environment, with fertile soil and plentiful hunting grounds, for the native Americans known as the Lenni Lenape.

In 1638, pioneers sailing from Sweden on two small ships, the Kalmar Nyckel and the Vogel Grip, came ashore and built a small community named Fort Christina, where they introduced both log houses and Lutheran church services to the New World.

In 1651, the Dutch established Fort Casimir seven miles to the south, in what is now New Castle. For nearly a quarter-century, the Swedes, Dutch, and English would battle for control of the land along the Delaware, with the English finally taking command in 1674.

In 1698, descendants of early Swedish and Finnish settlers built Holy Trinity (Old Swedes) Church near the site of Fort Christina. Holy Trinity remains today the nation's oldest church building still in use for worship with its original construction.

About a mile to the west, the area that would become the modern downtown Wilmington saw its first development in 1731. From the Christina north, Thomas Willing laid out streets in a grid pattern. From Water Street to the current Delaware Avenue (then called Kennett Road), from Walnut to West Streets, a map from the 1770s looked much like it does today. In 1739, when the new community of

Willingtown had about 600 residents, the Penn family gave it a charter and the name it retains today.

Over the ensuing two and a half centuries, ingenious thinkers and dedicated workers helped the City evolve from mill-town to shipbuilder, to chemical capital and, two decades ago, to a center for banking and finance.

While the gentle waters of the Christina enabled Wilmington to develop as a shipping center, Quaker settlers found the swift-flowing Brandywine ideal for powering flour mills. By the American Revolution, the Brandywine Superfine label had earned an international reputation for quality.

As the calendar turned from the 18th century to the 19th, three key events would portend the growing City's future. In 1795, Bank of Delaware, the state's first bank, was founded in Wilmington. Three years later, confident City fathers began constructing the Town Hall at Sixth and Market streets. Like the City, the building would endure, serving now as a museum operated by the Historical Society of Delaware. Then, in 1802, on the banks of the Brandywine northwest of the City, a family of French immigrants named du Pont began manufacturing gunpowder, changing Wilmington – and Delaware – forever.

As the DuPont Co. prospered in the 19th century, the Industrial Revolution spurred an evolution in Wilmington's economy. By 1838, the Philadelphia, Wilmington, and Baltimore Railroad linked the three cities. Soon the prime real estate along the tracks and the Christina became home to busy factories that turned out railroad cars, machinery, steam engines, and riverboats. In 1844, the Bangor, America's first iron-hulled propeller steamship, was launched in Wilmington.

At the same time, Wilmington became known for another type of railroad. Quaker merchant Thomas Garrett, befriended by abolitionist Harriet Tubman, opened his home at 227 Shipley Street to slaves heading north to freedom on the Underground Railroad. Although found guilty of harboring runaway slaves in 1848, Garrett never ceased his activities. Blacks in Wilmington revered Garrett as "Our Moses." He is credited with personally helping more than 2,700 slaves gain their freedom.

The post-Civil War era saw more progress. The Grand Opera House opened in 1871. Then came telephone lines, electric street lights, and electric street cars.

The turn of the century would bring two seismic shifts that shaped Wilmington's destiny.

In 1899, the Delaware General Assembly passed legislation making it easier for businesses to incorporate in Delaware than in other states. Big businesses did not have to move their headquarters and factories into the State to become a Delaware corporate citizen. Today, more than half the nation's publicly traded companies and 58 percent of the Fortune 500 have their corporate home in Delaware.

Then, in 1903, three young du Pont cousins – Pierre S., Alfred I. and T. Coleman – took control of the family business, built their headquarters at 10th and Market streets rather than move to Manhattan, and determined that chemicals had a future more promising than black powder. The chemical industry would soon dominate Wilmington, and the name DuPont would become synonymous with the City, and the State, for 75 years.

Indeed, the company's headquarters would also house the elegant Hotel du Pont and the Playhouse, whose stage would feature the best in theater, with shows on their way to Broadway or on tour after their run in the Big Apple was complete.

The du Pont family would express its largesse in many ways – supporting schools, highways, hospitals, libraries, and the arts in Wilmington and throughout the State.

World War I provided the impetus for the expansion of Wilmington's shipyards and the development of the $3 million Wilmington Marine Terminal at the mouth of the Christina. More jobs meant more housing, too – Union Park Gardens for the shipbuilders, Wawaset Park for the Du Pont executives.

Like many other cities, Wilmington experienced a decline following World War II, as suburban housing boomed and retailers abandoned downtown for suburban strip centers and malls. Wilmington's struggles prompted creative responses. The "urban homesteading" program of the 1970s produced a regentrification of some neighborhoods, notably Trinity Vicinity. The creation of the auto-free Market Street Mall made downtown pedestrian-friendly, but whatever stimulus it provided retailers was short-lived.

Oil embargoes, double-digit inflation, and international crises triggered a national manufacturing slump in the 1970s, driving some visionary leaders to consider new approaches to broaden the State's economy.

Wilmington Mayor William T. McLaughlin worked closely with Gov. Pierre S. du Pont IV to secure the passage of the Financial Center Development Act in 1981. This legislation, giving credit-card banks favorable tax treatment in exchange for creating new jobs, boosted employment in Wilmington and helped stabilize City and State revenue bases. MBNA would supplant DuPont as Wilmington's leading employer; Bank One, CitiBank and Juniper would become almost as familiar to locals as the venerable WSFS and Wilmington Trust,

As the curtain fell on the 20th century, rejuvenation of the Christina Riverfront would begin. After a 44-year absence, minor league baseball returned in 1993. With the Wilmington Blue Rocks playing in brand-new Frawley Stadium, an arts and convention center next door, and an outlet center across the parking lot, the riverfront became an appealing leisure destination. Then came new businesses – Juniper, ING Direct, AAA Mid-Atlantic, restaurants and nightclubs – allowing Wilmington to step into the 21st century full of optimism and pride as a new City began to emerge from the old.

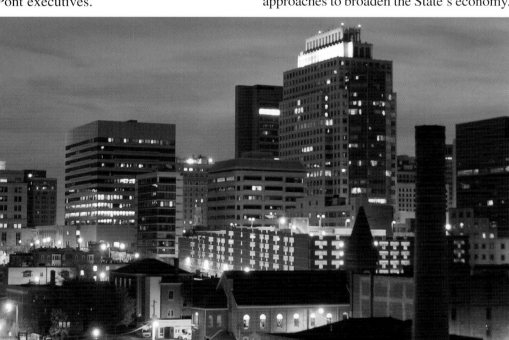

All photos by Paul Kennard

Delaware State Chamber of Commerce

Mission: To promote an economic climate that strengthens the competitiveness of Delaware businesses and benefits all citizens of the state.

The Delaware State Chamber of Commerce has a long history of advocating for business in Delaware. Founded in 1837 as the Wilmington Board of Trade, the State Chamber is older than even the U.S. Chamber of Commerce. As a matter of fact, when the U.S. Chamber got its start in 1912, the State Chamber was one of the original members.

Since its inception, the Chamber has supported businesses of all sizes. The founding members included a dry goods merchant, a carpenter, a physician and even two brothers who owned a hardware store. These small business owners were joined by some of the names that have become a part of Delaware history: Bancroft, Gilpin, and of course du Pont. This mix of sizes and sectors continues today.

As in present times, early Chamber members were active advocates for business. And some of the issues that they grappled with – taxes, education and economic development, for example – continue to occupy us today.

As early as 1872, the Chamber was lobbying for tax relief. In the early 1900s, the Chamber was involved in training public high school students for trades. Beginning in the late 1920s, the Chamber called for a bridge across the Delaware River to help economic development in the state. After more than two decades of lobbying, the Delaware Memorial Bridge opened in 1951. Fast forward to the end of the century. By the 1980s workers compensation costs had become a factor nationwide.

Today the Chamber remains involved in all of these issues and more on our members' behalf.

The State Chamber has 2,800 members that represent a wide variety of business sectors. Under the Chamber umbrella are five affiliates:

• The Small Business Alliance, the largest of the State Chamber's five affiliates, strives to improve the competitive position of Delaware small businesses. All businesses with 150 or fewer employees who are members of the State Chamber are automatically members of the Small Business Alliance. Led by its own Board of Managers, this group includes three committees that focus on benefits and services, legislative policy and education and development.

• Founded in 1856, the Delaware Manufacturing Association (DMA) is the local arm of the National Association of Manufacturers. All manufacturers who are members of the State Chamber are automatically members of the DMA. Led by a Board of Managers, its purpose is to recommend public policy initiatives that will foster a positive environment for manufacturers. There is a strong emphasis on environmental regulatory issues, infrastructure planning, workers' compensation, employee relations and science/technology education.

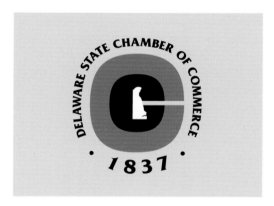

• The Delaware Retail Council (DRC) is the local arm of the National Retail Federation. In addition to advocating for retail interests in Legislative Hall, the DRC is the driving force behind the Retail Skills Center, a work force development and training program offered in partnership with Delaware Technical & Community College. The DRC and its members also support the community through such efforts as the Special Olympics Torch Run.

• The Partnership, Inc. is the State Chamber's education and work force development affiliate, helping to bridge the gap between business and education through such programs as Superstars in Education and Principal for a Day, as well as the Business Mentoring Task Force and summer career camps.

• The Delaware Public Policy Institute (DPPI) is a non-profit, non-partisan, non-governmental think tank that identifies emerging issues that drive Delaware's future public policy.

Diverse Membership

While the State Chamber counts Delaware's largest companies – MBNA, DuPont, Christiana Care, JPMorgan Chase and AstraZeneca – among its members, the vast majority of State Chamber members are companies with 150 employees or less. And more than half of DSCC member companies have fewer than 15 employees. Not only are small businesses the backbone of Delaware's economy, they are the heart of the State Chamber.

Regardless of their size, the State Chamber represents the interests of all of its members. It is the combined voices of all Chamber members that make the Chamber the strongest advocate for business in the state. When the business community speaks as one, it exerts a powerful influence.

A host of opportunities

Delaware's business community is blessed with a host of opportunities. We have a diverse economy and a motivated work force. Our court system has been ranked number one by the U.S. Chamber of Commerce for four years running and we are on solid financial footing. Our state balance sheet shows a strong surplus, giving policy makers the room to cut taxes and deal with rising workers' comp and health care costs, while still having enough money left over to fund priorities like public education and economic development. Our state's leaders, from the federal delegation on down, are committed to economic development.

We are lucky to enjoy an exceptional quality of life with world-class museums, a legacy of rich colonial history, diverse entertainment, great restaurants, and, of course, tax-free shopping.

A competitive edge

Delaware's businesses – indeed all businesses across the world – struggle to remain competitive and are always looking for a competitive edge. Through its political advocacy, work force development initiatives, cost-saving benefits and business-building initiatives, the Delaware State Chamber of Commerce provides employers with that edge.

Daisy Construction Company

Daisy Construction Company has had a long-standing business relationship with the City of Wilmington dating back to 1974 when Market Street was first converted from two-way traffic to a pedestrian mall. This relationship continues today with the recent completion of Phase II of the Market Street Streetscape Project. Streetscape is the term used to describe revitalization projects to enhance the appearance of urban areas, and improving the flow of vehicular traffic, as well as improving the infrastructure, such as underground utilities and storm water management systems. We are proud to have had an active role in Wilmington's renaissance. Daisy Construction has been involved in the revitalization of several areas of Wilmington, such as the Ships Tavern Project, Martin Luther King Boulevard, the Ship Yard Shops and Phase I of the Market Street Renovation Project. As a community-minded company; Daisy Construction hires its employees from the local areas where the projects are to be done. In this manner we are not only contributing to the local government by providing quality construction at the lowest possible price, we are also affording the local citizens gainful employment. We hire local area unskilled individuals as entry-level laborers. Many continue to apply themselves and rise up through the ranks to become heavy equipment operators and foremen. We fully recognize that what is good for Wilmington's growth and development is also good for Daisy Construction Company.

Leonard Iacono, president, founded Daisy Construction Company in 1973. Mr. Iacono started the business with two trucks and six employees. At that time the Company was known as Daisy Concrete. Today the company's operations include heavy highway construction, site development, asphalt and concrete paving, underground utilities and storm water management systems in both public and private sectors. The Company has grown from its humble beginnings to over 200 pieces or heavy construction equipment, 100 trucks and approximately 300 employees. Geographically the operations encompass projects in Delaware, Pennsylvania and Maryland.

With our continued growth in mind, in 2002 a second Delaware office was opened in Milton. Kent and Sussex counties are experiencing tremendous growth and as in Wilmington, we want to be part of that growth. We see exciting new projects springing up to serve the needs of business owners and to provide homes and shopping centers for families all across the state.

To maintain forward mobility in 2002 we extended our operations geographically into our nearby neighboring State of Maryland. We are now in the position to establish a permanent office in Baltimore County, replacing the temporary office in Aberdeen, MD.

Striving to stay abreast of this growth required changes in the way we think and conduct our business. This was accomplished by availing ourselves of the latest in equipment technology that gets

Market Street Reconstruction

the job done more efficiently and in less time. We are dedicated to investing our financial resources in recruiting the best and most knowledgeable people available. A proactive approach has kept Daisy Construction in the forefront of the new construction boom in highway and site development. We have also established ourselves in the construction community by not only providing high quality work, but also offering site-planning services to owners and developers. By drawing on our wealth of knowledge and experience we are able to maximize on established budgets and schedules as well as avoiding costly mistakes. Substantial savings can be realized by proper planning of the development phase of any project. We work in tandem with owners and developers; always researching their projects for alternative constructions methods and materials to lower construction costs.

Construction has changed drastically over the years. Contractors now have to be better educated and have had to place engineers and accountants on their staff. It takes a team of talented people several days or weeks just to put a bid together. Henry Kissinger once said, "Success only buys you an admission ticket to more problems." This is never truer than when considering construction of a highway or a building. Problems and challenges are presented from hour to hour in the construction business. We understand that owners and developers look to their contractor to solve their problems, not become one.

Construction and/or maintaining a highway present unique problems and challenges. The roadway must remain open, affording a continuous flow of traffic while replacing the roadway one lane at a time. This requires careful and detailed

Market Street Today

planning that can takes years before construction actually starts. Public safety is always a big consideration, both for the motoring public and the workers. Safeguards built into the project such as concrete barriers, warning signs, closed lanes, flaggers and traffic pylons often are just a source of frustration to the general public. However, you can't make the roads and highways better without some inconvenience. The next time you are delayed in traffic due to highway construction, keep your cool, your personal safety and the safety of the workers in mind. They want to go home to their families at the end of the day too.

Diamond Technologies, Inc.

Diamond Technologies was founded in Wilmington, Delaware in 1996 and is proud to be a part of the Wilmington renaissance. During its short history the company has rapidly established itself as one of Delaware's leading Information Technology innovators. The company prides itself on helping organizations achieve their strategic business objectives through the implementation of leading information technologies. By working with a wide range of large and medium-sized organizations in specific industries, Diamond Technologies has learned what works and what doesn't.

Diamond Technologies provides a comprehensive range of information technology services including Application Development & Integration, Web Solutions, Network & System Services, Database Solutions and Hosting & Managed Services. The company has delivered real-world solutions to prestigious clients in a variety of industries including Government, Banking & Financial Services, Insurance, Gaming & Entertainment and Pharmaceuticals. Diamond Technologies' approach is designed to meet the diverse needs of its clients, from providing comprehensive management of the entire project life cycle to providing specialized resources to complement its client's teams. Diamond Technologies employs a full time staff from the local area, providing highly competitive salaries and comprehensive benefits, including ongoing professional training. At a time when many IT jobs are moving off shore, the company takes pride in being a local provider of high quality services and jobs in the Delaware business community.

Diamond Technologies' company culture embodies a passion for satisfying its clients and its employees. Its guiding philosophies are centered on the principles of: Advocating a passion for client satisfaction in all aspects of its technical services and business practices; Assisting organizations in achieving their strategic business objectives through the successful application of information technology; Providing a work environment that embodies technical excellence, professionalism, ethics, teamwork, and continued career advancement; and promoting company growth and prosperity for the continued reward and development of the entire organization.

Throughout its history Diamond Technologies has been the recipient of numerous awards and recognition, including a "Best in the Business" award from the Wilmington News Journal, "Inc. 500" and "Philadelphia 100" awards, "Delaware's Small Business of the Year" award from the United States Small Business Administration and recognition by Delaware Today magazine as one of the "Best Places to Work" in Delaware.

A socially minded organization that believes in giving back to the community, Diamond Technologies contributes both through direct financial contributions and through the active participation of its leadership and employees. The company serves as an active Technology Partner to the Appoquinimink School District in New Castle County by providing scholarship dollars and technology consulting assistance to the District. The company encourages its staff to participate in community related activities and organizations. As a result, members of its staff are actively involved in a broad range of organizations, including Junior Achievement, The United Way, The Young Marines, Little League Baseball, Superstars In Education, and many others.

The Port of Wilmington, Delaware

In 1923, the City of Wilmington had the foresight to create a deepwater port on the Christina River and to forever more link its economic future to domestic and foreign commerce. Although the Port of Wilmington, Delaware was originally formed to service regional logistics needs, cargoes arriving at the Port today support consumer demand in cities and states over one thousand miles distant from the Delaware Valley. The Port, international commerce and domestic logistics have created a synergy that has benefited the entire region through job creation, in supporting the development of industries relying on international trade and in establishing a strong revenue and tax base.

To keep the Port well capitalized from both an infrastructure and financial perspective and to take advantage of future cargo opportunities, the City of Wilmington agreed to transfer ownership of the Port to the State of Delaware in 1995. The Governor of Delaware established the Diamond State Port Corporation in 1996 to manage the Port, its business growth and its fiscal operations. Since 1996, the State has invested over

$120 million in new warehouses, pier development and cargo handling equipment.

The Port is located at the confluence of the Christina and Delaware Rivers and approximately 60 miles from the Atlantic Ocean. It encompasses 360 acres, has seven deep-water general cargo berths with over 4000 lineal feet of pier space, an

oil transfer jetty, and a newly constructed 875-foot long auto and Ro-Ro berth on the Delaware River. Two high speed, multi purpose gantry cranes and one heavy lift crane are used to load and discharge the five million tons of cargo moving through the Port each year. Truckers have ready access to all major interstate highways and major domestic railroads provide efficient and competitively priced rail service.

A diversified cargo portfolio, a port managed terminal and warehouse operation and a tenant base that includes Dole Fresh Fruit Company, Chiquita Fresh North America, Volkswagen of America and Citrosuco North America Inc. have sustained the Port's growth and profitability. However, in the end it is our strong, flexible and commercially minded work force and their teamwork that has earned Wilmington's its brand as "The Port of Personal Service". The Port's focus on developing partnerships with our customers and on solving their logistics needs will continue to serve well both the City of Wilmington and the State of Delaware long into the future.

Citrosuco North America, Inc.

Citrosuco North America, Inc. has maintained a strong and mutually beneficial association with the Wilmington area for many years. As part of the Fischer Group, one of Brazil's largest multi-national agribusiness conglomerates, Citrosuco, the Group's largest business unit, is one of the leading World Wide orange juice processors, operating processing plants in Brazil and Florida as well as their own fleet of ships and distribution terminals in the United States, Europe and Asia.

Based in Lake Wales, Florida, Citrosuco North America, Inc. chose The Port of Wilmington as the home of their distribution center to serve their northeastern customer base. From here we distribute juice products to major branded and private label packagers throughout the United States and Canada.

The choice was easy – The Port of Wilmington is a full-service deepwater port and marine terminal, located at the confluence of the Delaware and Christina Rivers, 65 miles from the Atlantic Ocean. Since it was founded in 1923, the Port of Wilmington has been a major Mid-Atlantic import/export gateway for a wide variety of maritime cargoes and trade. It has been consistently ranked as one of the leaders in the import of concentrate juices, fresh fruit, bananas, and capacity for dock-side cold storage. In Wilmington we have an established port facility location for our distribution tankfarm situated in a major northeastern metropolitan center conveniently located along the Route 95 corridor providing great access to a variety of inland transportation channels. The location provides us with an established infrastructure and access to a variety of business services.

The City of Wilmington also offers the best of all worlds. The greater Wilmington area provides Citrosuco with a talented and plentiful labor force upon which to draw for broad based skills and abilities. We consider our employees to be one of our greatest strengths and are proud that many of our Wilmington employees have spent most of their careers with Citrosuco. Wilmington is a business friendly city and offers its residents an outstanding combination of historical, cultural and recreational opportunities unique to the area and easily accessible.

Located midway between New York City and Washington, DC, and just 30 minutes south of Philadelphia, Wilmington, at a population of approximately 72,000, is just the right size – a city with all of the amenities and none of the headaches of big city life. Residents can easily access everything from world class beaches and outdoor recreational events to cutting edge medical facilities and educational institutions. As the county seat of New Castle County, Wilmington is at the center of attention for area government and is the gateway to the Brandywine Valley's world-class museums, gardens and cultural attractions.

For Citrosuco North America, Inc., the choice was easy, we choose Wilmington!

One of the company's Orange Juice carriers, the Premium do Brasil, sails into Port of Wilmington

Murphy Marine Services, Inc.

Murphy Marine Services, Inc.

has maintained a strong presence on the Wilmington waterfront for more than 25 years. With a close proximity to the Atlantic Ocean (30 miles) and a strong partnership with the Delaware State Port Corporation (DSPC) and the International Longshoreman Association (ILA), Murphy Marine has been able to provide a whole range of expert services to the industry leaders it serves in Wilmington.

These expert services are dominated by Stevedoring (loading and unloading cargo from ocean-going ships) and includes expertise with:
• Containerized Cargo
• Break-Bulk Cargo
• Automotive (Ro-Ro) Cargo
• Bulk Cargo

In addition, Murphy Marine provides Management and Administrative Services which include:
• Management of the Maintenance and Repair Shops for major customers
• Management of the Trailer Interchange Receipt gates for major customers
• Safety and Accident Prevention
• Labor negotiations
• Liaison with the Port Authority
• Payroll Services for more than 900 employees - union and management
• Insurance Management

Murphy Marine provides a wide range of Containerized Cargo handling services for a variety of multi-national major customers.

In this part of its business, Murphy Marine handles approximately 230,000 TEU'S and 1,300,000 tons of containerized cargoes each year.

The handing of Break-Bulk cargo for customers who ship from throughout the world is another part of the Murphy Marine expertise.

Murphy Marine handles in excess of 300,000 pallets and 500,000 tons of a variety of break-bulk products each year.

Murphy Marine expertly handles a variety of Automotive (Ro-Ro) cargoes for its major international customers.

Murphy Marine handles between 75,000 and 150,000 autos each year.

Murphy Marine has the capability and expertise to handle a wide range of Bulk cargoes from Coal to Fertilizer.

Murphy Marine handled in excess of 100,000 tons of bulk products in 2004 and has the capacity to handle a least 500,000 tons of bulk products annually.

Murphy Marine Services, with its full staff of extremely hands-on, experienced and expert Ship Superintendents and its expert Administrative Management group, has a team which is poised to grow the City and Port of Wilmington in the 21st century.

M. Davis & Sons Inc.

When Edward R. Davis began a small tinsmithing business in 1870, he forged the beginnings of a company that would span five generations to become a leading provider of fully integrated industrial, commercial, and pharmaceutical contracting services known throughout the Delaware Valley.

M. Davis is proud of its history of quality workmanship, commitment to the highest standards of customer service and workplace safety that began with its founder more than a century ago.

Edward R. Davis first established a shop on Lovering Avenue in Wilmington, relying mostly on residential roof repair as the mainstay of his business; although, he also repaired household products. At the turn of the century, he moved his business to a shop located on Lincoln Street. There, he sold cook stoves, kerosene stoves, warm air furnaces, oil lamps, smoke pipes and hardware for these products. By this time, Edward had also begun to change the course of the company. With a crew of 30 men, the small shop began to provide mechanical services, such as ductwork installation, to other local industries, namely Bancroft Textile Mills.

His son, Marcellus Davis Sr., for whom the company is now named, took the reins in 1912 and continued to sell household goods at the shop until 1920. Following his father's lead, Marcellus Sr. chose to expand the business by directing his crews to craft products and provide services for local textile mills and a local brewery. In 1931, he moved the business once more to Silverside Road and its primary customer was Doeskin Paper. In 1946, his son, Marcellus "Pete" Davis Jr., procured the business and kept it focused on serving local paper mills and providing heating and cooling services.

Today, Pete's son, Charles R. Davis, and granddaughter, Margaret "Peg" DelFabbro, carry on the company's original mission to provide superior services at a fair price, guided by the philosophy that quality is never an accident – it is the result of attention to detail and a sincere effort by everyone involved.

What began as a modest trades business in 1870 has evolved into a growing enterprise employing more than 300 highly skilled and licensed craftsmen: crane operators, welders, riggers, pipe-fitters, millwrights, and machinists and electricians. This diverse, multi-craft workforce provides a full range of the highest quality industrial, commercial and pharmaceutical building services.

The M. Davis and Sons' Fabrication Shop, located at 200 Hadco Road in Wilmington, is a complete turnkey operation offering specialty sheet metal fabrication, repairs to ASME Code Section I boilers/pipe, Section VIII vessels/tanks, columns and reactors, and

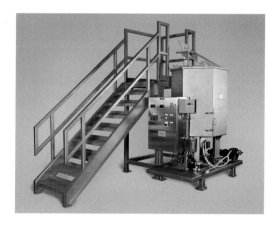

manufacture of process skids. A team of draftsmen use the latest in computer technology to design and specify various types of equipment and processing systems.

M. Davis & Sons' electrical professionals are licensed in Delaware, Maryland, Pennsylvania, New Jersey, Tennessee, Virginia and West Virginia, and are continually branching out to other areas of the country. Our electrical group provides quality electrical renovations, plant maintenance, branch circuits, troubleshooting, data wiring, high voltage load breaks, heat tracing and 64 KV installations. Custom designing and building control panels, including UL panels, is our specialty.

While M. Davis & Sons continues to service many types of industries, there is now a new focus on serving pharmaceutical, bio-technology, food and beverage, and FDA regulated facilities. The M. Davis Team can provide design, custom fabrication, construction and installation of equipment, including electrical assemblies, troubleshooting and maintenance to these industries. Our commitment to our customer is to provide fully integrated, quality services, with maximum production efficiency, in a work safe environment and adherence to budgets.

To date, M. Davis has served such prestigious companies as Hynetics Inc., DuPont Merck & Company, Alfa Laval, Centocor, Baxter Healthcare, Dietz and Watson, Frito-Lay and Proctor & Gamble. Our proven quality of performance and service for these companies has led to additional work beyond the Mid-Atlantic region in states such as Texas, Missouri, Tennessee, Kentucky, Virginia, West Virginia, New York, and Rhode Island.

Just as we pride ourselves on our performance, we also pride ourselves on maintaining safety practices that meet and exceed industry and OSHA standards and our customers' expectations. The practice of work place safety is built into every job we do and is second nature to our workforce. M. Davis has been recognized for its exemplary safety practices as a recipient of the Association of Builders and Contractors Platinum Safety Award and The DuPont Safety Award.

Our Team believes there is no job worth doing, unless it is done exceptionally well.

The Buccini/Pollin Group, Inc.

The Buccini/Pollin Group, Inc. (BPG) is a privately-held full-service real estate acquisition, development and management company headquartered in Wilmington, DE, with offices in Washington, DC, and New York City. Formed in 1993, BPG has developed and acquired office, hotel, residential, industrial and R&D, retail and parking properties in the Mid-Atlantic and Northeastern regions of the United States.

The principals of BPG take a unique, hands-on approach to all aspects of the company's operations. BPG affiliates oversee all aspects of project financing, construction, leasing, operations and disposition of its real estate assets in order to maximize financial returns. The full service approach gives BPG control of its portfolio's future.

BPG has been one of the biggest cheerleaders and largest investors in the City of Wilmington over the past five years. In 1999, BPG purchased three buildings totaling over one million square feet from the DuPont Company. During the following three years, BPG completed a total renovation of the Brandywine and Nemours buildings, converting them into class A office space which is now home to some of the most prestigious office and retail tenants in the State of Delaware.

BPG became the pioneer of downtown living in Wilmington with its renovation of the former Delaware Trust Building. BPG made a significant investment in Wilmington's Renaissance with this project. BPG purchased the vacant building in 2002 and immediately commenced the redevelopment of the historic bank building into a luxury residential and retail complex. By 2003, the building was open for business and was an immediate success. Today there are over five hundred residents living in downtown Wilmington in the building now named The Residences at Rodney Square.

BPG's follow-up development is transforming the banks of Wilmington's Christina River. A forgotten 8-acre parcel of land situated on the southern edge of the River has been transformed into townhomes, luxury apartments and condominium high-rises. These are the first luxury residential towers ever built in downtown Wilmington and will be home to nearly 750 new residents to the City of Wilmington.

BPG is proud to continue its support of Wilmington, its home.

Early stages of construction, Christina Landing

The Brandywine Building at night

The Nemours Building

St. Francis Hospital

▲ *St. Francis Hospital, Wilmington, Delaware*

Specialized Medicine with a Human Touch

St. Francis Hospital, Delaware's only Catholic hospital, was founded by the Sisters of St. Francis of Philadelphia in 1924. The Sisters have been actively engaged in healthcare ministering since their foundress, Mother Francis Bachmann, opened the congregation's first hospital in 1855. The mission of St. Francis is, as a member of Catholic Health East, under the sponsorship of Hope ministries, to be a compassionate,

healing presence in the communities we serve. We continue in the tradition of our founders, the Sisters of St. Francis of Philadelphia. The Core Values are: Reverence for each person, Community, Justice, Commitment to the poor, Stewardship, Courage and Integrity.

The hospital is located at 7th and Clayton Streets in Wilmington and is presently licensed for 395 beds. The campus consists of the DuPont Building, which was completed in 1937, the main hospital building, which was completed in 1975 and replaced the original hospital building, the Medical Office Building, added in the early 1980s, and the Medical Services Building, constructed in 1992. The hospital provides a wide array of

services, including emergency care, cardiac care, acute care and numerous outpatient services.

In October 2002, St. Francis launched the region's most comprehensive, state-of-the-art Open Heart program as part of its $20 million, five-year Master Facility Plan. The St. Francis Heart Center provides a full range of cardiac services, from expanded cardiac catheterization services to a broad range of treatment options, including bypass and other surgery and rehabilitation.

In July 2004 the new 29-bed, 60-percent larger St. Francis Emergency Department opened. The new department features two state-of-the-art critical care/trauma rooms and larger, private rooms with the latest

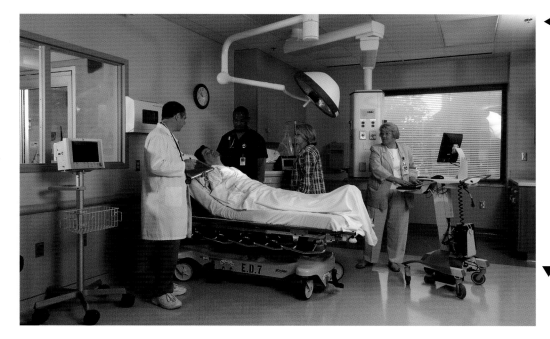

equipment and monitoring. It is located near the Intensive Care Unit, Operating Rooms, Cardiac Catheterization Lab, and latest CT scanning technology, providing easy access for patients and staff to other necessary medical services. The department is operational 24 hours a day/seven days a week, and part of the Delaware Trauma System.

St. Francis is a full-service community hospital, and women's health is one of its specialties. St. Francis offers its Family Birthplace with a level-two neonatal intensive care unit, as well as classes in labor, delivery, breastfeeding and caring for newborns.

St. Francis also has advanced breast care and diagnostic capabilities. The ImageChecker®, technology that double-checks mammograms, helps St. Francis radiologists locate suspicious areas.

St. Francis "pioneered" the ImageChecker technology, as it was the first hospital on the East Coast to use it. St. Francis offers comprehensive women's services at the hospital and also at its North Wilmington Women's Center located on Foulk Road.

St. Francis' 20-bed Intensive Care Unit features leading-edge technology. Power columns permit 360-degree access to the patient. Spacious rooms and expanded visitor areas offer the utmost in comfort and technology to patients and visitors. In addition, the ICU was the only Delaware ICU named one of the Top 100 Hospitals ICUs in a survey by Solucient Leadership Institute.

Other areas and amenities include home care services, neurosurgery, award-winning orthopedics, a pain center, travel medicine, a skilled nursing unit, dialysis, lithotripsy,

sleep/neurodiagnostics center and GI Lab. The hospital offers community-oriented programs such as basic life support and pre-operative classes to educate patients about joint replacement surgery and rehabilitation.

Another vital part of the healthcare system is the Franciscan Care Center at Brackenville located in Hockessin. The center provides long-term care and restorative nursing care, along with rehabilitation services. Community outreach efforts consist of the Center of Hope, a family practice center in Newark, the Tiny Steps prenatal program for low-income pregnant women, and the St. Clare Van, which provides medical care to the underserved and uninsured. New initiatives at the hospital include bariatric surgery and expansion of services for cancer patients.

Hercules Incorporated

Now in its ninth decade of operation, Hercules Incorporated has been a leading business presence in Wilmington, Delaware since its founding in 1912 as Hercules Powder Company, the result of a spin-off from DuPont.

Our company has gone through many transformations since then – from providing explosives for our allied forces for two major world wars to a time when it made

citizen and member of the communities in which our employees live and work.

When Hercules decided to build its permanent corporate headquarters in 1980 many options were evaluated. The City of Wilmington, together with the State of Delaware, worked on proposals and architectural concepts to help Hercules find an appropriate building site. While considering various sites, Hercules was aware of its

many corporate and community events through the years.

Bounded by Market, 13th and Orange Streets, Hercules Plaza was a forerunner in the revitalization of downtown Wilmington and the keystone of the Brandywine Gateway.

During the time Hercules has been in downtown Wilmington, there have been many changes to the skyline and the business

plastics and rocket fuels to today. Today, Hercules is a premier global specialty chemicals company with four businesses – Pulp and Paper, Aqualon, FiberVisions, and Pinova.

The specialty chemicals we produce go into everyday products that people rely on to make their lives more healthy, more convenient and more enjoyable. They enhance the performance, quality and durability of products such as baby diapers, writing paper, paper towels, paint, milk and juice containers, hair shampoo, toothpaste, sports drinks and chewing gum.

As a maker of chemicals and a Responsible Care Company®, Hercules is committed to operating in a safe and environmentally friendly manner. We also strive to be a good corporate

role as a major resident of the City of Wilmington and the advantages of remaining downtown, including transportation of employees to and from work.

The groundbreaking ceremony for the Plaza took place on October 6, 1980. In June of 1983 dedication ceremonies were held for Hercules new Corporate Headquarters Building.

Today, Hercules Plaza is a well-recognized landmark in Wilmington. Its graceful main entrance faces south toward downtown Wilmington, while its reflective façade overlooks the Brandywine River from the rear of the building. The 200-foot-high, 90-foot-square atrium houses over 4,000 plants, bringing an outdoor environment inside. A waterfall cascading through the center of the atrium creates a serene, natural setting that has been the venue for

environment. One thing that always remains constant is the need for solid corporate/community relationships, coupled with strong employee volunteer participation.

Hercules employees have always shown a high degree of support and commitment to their communities. They give of their time as volunteers at food banks, homeless shelters, hospitals and schools. They participate in company-sponsored events for organizations such as the United Way, Easter Seals, the American Heart Association, The American Cancer Society, Multiple Sclerosis, The Salvation Army, Meals on Wheels and other worthy causes. Whatever the call, they respond generously.

On behalf of the employees at Hercules, we are proud to be part of the community and spirit of Wilmington.

CAI

CAI, founded in 1981, is an Information Technology (IT) consulting and outsourcing services organization. Clients include organizations in the private sector from Fortune 1000 companies to smaller companies with significant IT requirements, federal, state and local government agencies, and institutions of higher education. Employing over 700 associates out of its Wilmington operations office, CAI focuses on world class service and customer satisfaction while promoting a positive work environment and culture.

CAI offers a broad spectrum of IT services including Consulting, Application Development, Application Services, Desktop Services, Software Testing, and E-commerce solutions in both managed services and staff augmentation environments. CAI enables its clients to increase efficiency, and reduce cost through proprietary processes and methodology in IT operational excellence. This approach allows CAI to meet each customer's individual requirements and deliver projects with the highest degree of improved productivity. Working closely with clients and listening to their needs gives CAI the ability to offer customized solutions that are delivered on time and in budget. The company operates on the belief that regardless of industry or size, clients should expect high quality, cost effective, and timely IT solutions.

Headquartered in Allentown, Pennsylvania, CAI has a worldwide presence with over 40 offices in North America, Europe and Asia. The Delaware Valley operation, headquartered in Wilmington, is the largest of CAI's three regions. With humble beginnings in Managing Director Ernie Dianastasis' living room, the business grew and the operation moved to its first office in Chadds Ford, Pennsylvania. Driven by significant growth in the 1980's, the regional headquarters relocated to its current 901 Market Street facilities in downtown Wilmington in 1990.

CAI's unique entrepreneurial culture is committed to providing a work environment advocating personal and professional growth. Devoid of "status-ism" and bureaucracy, the company's success is determined by the achievements of each associate. As such, CAI fosters an environment of mutual respect and encourages individuals to challenge the status quo. This ensures the continual improvement of business and business processes and is one reason CAI's retention rate is well above industry standards. Service offerings are founded on the acknowledgement that associates are a critical resource for success.

CAI is consistently recognized as a leader committed to the growth and development of the community in which it serves. CAI associates participate in many activities and organizations within the community such as mentoring, Habitat for Humanity, The Boys & Girls Club of Delaware, the Delmarva Blood Bank, The Grand Opera House, The Delaware Community Foundation, and many others. In 2005 CAI became the title sponsor for the annual Easter Seals Volleyball Tournament which raised over $ 200,000 for this worthy cause. In addition, CAI also offers technical expertise to arts organizations, donates computers and software to schools and makes financial donations to a wide variety of community based programs, while making it easy for its associates to volunteer their time in the community. These activities foster a unique opportunity for CAI associates to serve as community leaders, in and out of the office.

This exceptional view of volunteerism helped CAI gain the title of News Journal's "Business the Business" for Community Service in 2004. As a responsible corporate citizen, CAI is passionate about supporting cultural activities and regional wellness.

Over the past several years CAI has also become an active member of the business community. Ernie Dianastasis is a member of the Delaware Business Roundtable, the Delaware State Chamber of Commerce, and serves as Chair of the Council on Competitiveness Delaware Entrepreneurial Action Group. He is also in a member of the Governor's Strategic Economic Council. These efforts are focused on continuing to drive economic growth in the city of Wilmington, the state of Delaware and the region.

For over two decades, CAI has offered world class service to clients in the Delaware Valley and beyond out of its Wilmington office. Working alongside community leaders and forging a bond between public and private sector is fast becoming a hallmark for CAI and its business. CAI exemplifies how a local business can prosper while making a lasting impression in its community.

Wilmington College

Wilmington College shares more than just a name with the great city of Wilmington; it shares a long-term vision of revitalization and growth. Just as the city has witnessed sweeping changes to the Christina Riverfront, a vast improvement in transportation, construction of the Shipyard shops and beautification of the area, Wilmington College has continued to expand its resources. This is made evident with the opening of two new state-of-the-art facilities in a mere eight-month span: the Wilson Graduate Center in New Castle and the spacious new building with classic appeal in Dover. Wilmington College is proud to be a part of the city of Wilmington and proud to contribute to its success by offering equal opportunities for higher learning.

In 1981, Wilmington College acquired the U.S. Customs House at Sixth and King streets. Built in 1841, the gracious classic revival building was one of Wilmington's architectural jewels and would eventually house Wilmington College's Graduate Center.

The Commonwealth Group

The Commonwealth Group is a fully integrated and diversified real estate company – and one of the largest enterprises of its kind in Delaware. The privately held, family owned and operated business provides a comprehensive portfolio of services to its clients. These services include real estate investment development, acquisition/disposition, construction management, property management, leasing and marketing. Projects are located throughout Delaware, Pennsylvania, Maryland, Colorado and California.

The company, more than 50 years old, has involved the expertise of three generations. It was established in 1936 by Benjamin Vinton Sr. to oversee the investments of those who had financial interests in oil and gas companies in the west. In 1945, during its second generation of ownership and management, Commonwealth ventured into real estate and gradually developed a solid track record for innovative, cost effective commercial projects. Brock J. Vinton, the current President and CEO, took yet another step forward in 1978 when he merged several entities into what is now known as The Commonwealth Group, creating the full service real estate company that today is active in over $500 million dollars of real estate development and construction.

While maintaining a large presence in the suburbs with projects such as the New Castle Corporate Commons, Riveredge Industrial Park and The Mill at White Clay Creek, the company made a commitment to the redevelopment of the City and in December of 2002, relocated its headquarters to the Wilmington Riverfront. This move would allow the company to closely monitor its current projects in the City including the new AAA Headquarters located on the Riverfront and The Renaissance Centre.

The recently completed AAA Mid-Atlantic Headquarters building was designed to embody the history of the Riverfront and the industrial age architecture of the surrounding buildings. The six stories of old world style brick with glass additions gives the impression that this is a building that has endured the years while being retrofitted and expanded through the 20th century.

The Renaissance Centre, Wilmington's first new office building since the late 1980's, encompasses an entire city block and includes a 170,000 square foot office tower, a 350 car parking garage and the restoration of the building facades of historic Market Street into 35,000 square feet of revitalized office, retail and residential components. The project, located across the street from the Justice Center will become the bridge between the Central Business District and the ongoing revitalization efforts at the Riverfront and Ships Tavern Districts.

The Commonwealth Group takes great pride in the ability to develop buildings that are not only functional but are appealing and sensitive to the history and surrounding environment in which they are built. As a distinguished leader in commercial real estate development, the attributes that distinguish Commonwealth are the ingenuity and creativity the firm brings to the numerous challenges inherent in every project.

Located on the Wilmington Riverfront, the recently completed AAA Mid-Atlantic Headquarters brings 350 new jobs to the City.

The Renaissance Centre, slated for completion in the fall of 2006, will revitalize a once dilapidated city block with office, retail and residential opportunities.

Jackson Cross Partners

OUR GUIDING PRINCIPLES

RESPECT EACH INDIVIDUAL
WE ENCOUNTER.
DISTINGUISH OURSELVES BY THE
QUALITY OF OUR WORK.
UPHOLD OUR REPUTATION
FOR **INTEGRITY.**

There are many critical points in the life cycle of owning or occupying a property. The financial and operational impact of decisions made at those critical points can deeply affect the success of an enterprise. That's why Jackson Cross Partners has developed a comprehensive service platform that provides clear vision at every point of intersection.

Knowledge Assembly

Because making proactive and informed decisions regarding commercial real estate cannot be done without accurate and timely information, Jackson Cross has developed a process-centered approach to information gathering and management that fully enhances strategic real estate decision-making, as a key element to your overall business plan.

Planning & Analysis

At Jackson Cross, our artful application of technology allows us to bring a different perspective – a critical and analytical view, with creative solutions – to the challenges presented in each project, while helping you evaluate the optimal strategy going forward.

Project Execution

Once a plan is implemented, it is critical to provide the skills, resources and single point-of-control to ensure successful execution. Our market specialization, resources and experience provide the deal-making skills and business savy to deliver consistently exceptional results.

Continuing Management

Jackson Cross is committed to your success every day – not just the day the deal is done. The Jackson Cross Way creates a partnership, which allows us to regularly consult with you so we can proactively identify opportunities to adjust your real estate plan to changing business demands.

MARKETS SERVED

Jackson Cross Partners offers comprehensive market coverage throughout the Metropolitan Philadelphia area. With offices in Pennsylvania, Delaware and New Jersey, as well as strategic partnerships throughout the world, we can service large and small corporations, and real estate investors and developers – wherever their needs may arise. Our process-centered approach is fully exportable to other markets and we have regularly directed projects for clients in cities throughout North America and Europe. And, our affiliation with ONCOR International and the Society of Industrial and Office Realtors (SIOR) allows us immediate access to current market intelligence in more than 200 cities worldwide and local resources to augment our project team.

JACKSON CROSS
PARTNERS

Serving Delaware, Pennsylvania and New Jersey

An affiliate of NorthMarq Captial

Contact us at www.jcrosspartners.com
302-792-1301 or 610-265-7700

Cover & Rossiter

Cover & Rossiter is one of Delaware's oldest and most respected public accounting firms. Founded in 1939 by Clarence A. Cover as the original Wilmington office of McConnell and Breiden of Philadelphia, the firm has established and nurtured trusted and long-standing relationships with many of the area's most prominent businesses, organizations and individuals.

The history of Cover & Rossiter is very much entwined with the growth and development of the Wilmington region. Over the past 75 years, the firm has moved and expanded in keeping with the changing business and residential climate and demographics. Originally located at 9th and Orange Streets in downtown Wilmington, Cover & Rossiter has maintained offices in North Wilmington, Montchanin and now in its present location in Wilmington near Rockford Park. Regardless of its office location, the firm has been committed to serving the current and emerging needs of its clients throughout the Wilmington area.

The firm has grown in size and capability as well. Our emphasis has always been on providing personal and responsive service grounded in sound, individualized advice – a formula that has enabled our consistent growth. Beginning with a handful of employees, the firm is now comprised of approximately 40 people with a breadth of experience and capability that is second to none. Our current partners – Kathleen D. Wilhere, Geoff Langdon and Diane M. Burke – remain dedicated to our history and commitment of service. And one of our greatest successes has been assisting many of the area's leading businesses, organizations, families and individuals to succeed in their endeavors, thereby strengthening the quality of life in the Wilmington area.

While our rich heritage certainly gives us a deep sense of tradition and experience, today's Cover & Rossiter is anything but traditional. The firm now provides a full range of accounting and advisory services: auditing services, investment holding company services, corporate tax services, personal tax services, trust and estate services, litigation support and forensic accounting services, financial planning and investment advisory services, small business accounting services and international tax services.

For our employees, Wilmington is much more than a place to work – it is a place to be involved! The members of the firm have taken great pride in being active in the community. Associates routinely give of their time and talents to participate in numerous walk-a-thons, charity events, and service organizations, such as the Wilmington Rotary Club and Wilmington Jaycees. Members of the firm also add their expertise by serving on the boards of directors of local organizations, including the A.I. duPont Hospital for Children, West End Neighborhood House and Cornerstone West.

They also reach out to educate students and professionals alike. In education, the firm's partners have taught courses in accounting, management and finance at the University of Delaware and Goldey-Beacom College. Our associates are also frequent guest lecturers at local colleges and professional associations and contributors of articles in publications of financial, tax or general interest.

Maintaining professional skills and development is another passion of our associates, who are active participants as officers or members in many leading accounting associations, including the American Institute of Certified Public Accountants, Delaware Society of Certified Public Accountants, American Board of Forensic Accountants, Wilmington Tax Group and the Estate Planning Council of Delaware. Several of our associates are past graduates of the Leadership Delaware program.

As we conclude our first 75 years, we remain energized and optimistic about the future of our community and our firm. It is with great pride that Cover & Rossiter has and will continue to serve the needs of clients in our birthplace – *the City of Wilmington!*

COVER & ROSSITER

Certified Public Accountants & Advisors

Emory Hill

Emory Hill is a fully integrated Real Estate Company with the resources to design, build, finance, lease, and maintain commercial, industrial, and residential properties. The company was founded in 1981 by Robert H. Hill and R. Clayton Emory. Carmen J. Facciolo, Jr. joined in 1983 and became a partner that year.

For over 24 years, Emory Hill has been a major player in the greater Wilmington real estate arena, developing projects like the Little Falls Centre, the White Clay Center, and Pencader Corporate Center, to name just a few. The company built its reputation on development and construction and completed over 12 million square feet of office, industrial, flex, retail and residential space with a value of approximately $850 million.

Throughout the years, Emory Hill has had the flexibility to adjust to the changing requirements of the market, shifting its emphasis from development to providing comprehensive real estate services to a growing number of outside clients, and investors. Today, a large part of our revenue is derived from brokerage, construction, property management, and maintenance services for third party clients. What has not changed, however, is Emory Hill's owner perspective. We build to last, and we manage every property like it is our own.

Pencader XI

In 1989, Emory Hill Real Estate Services, Inc. was established to independently handle Brokerage, Property Management, and Maintenance. In 1997, our Brokerage Services were further strengthened by joining NAI, the largest global partnership of real estate service

Abby Medical Center

providers. This alliance resulted in enhanced services that include sales and acquisitions, leasing and marketing, and financial services. Marketing tools such as financial analysis, site mapping, demographic targeting and an extensive prospect and property database have dramatically increased the company's reach and exposure and provide a competitive edge for our brokers. We have attracted many Fortune 500 clients and government agencies and lease an average of one million square feet per year with a volume of approximately $200 million. In addition, we have extensive investment experience and have financed over 1.5 billion dollars of real estate, including construction loans, permanent financing, participating debt and joint venture structures.

Emory Hill and Company's full service construction management services have the ability to take a job from the planning stages through occupancy and beyond. Recently completed projects include the renovation of a center city historical building for the Delaware State Bar Association, student housing for Washington College, new construction of several medical facilities such as the Abby Medical Center, renovation of the old Wanamaker building for Accenture, interior fit outs for Bank One and Blue Cross Blue Shield, industrial structures for Integris Metals, and Staples, the Pencader XI Building, and several award winning retail centers. Our in-house team of experienced construction professionals, on-site management, and flexible delivery methods allow us to consistently deliver an attractive product built with pride. "On time and on budget" is not just a promise at Emory Hill; it is a fundamental component of our management process.

The Property Management Department oversees the administration of all aspects of the lease document and evaluates and maintains the healthy performance of each investment. The department now manages approximately 61 commercial properties with 350 tenants and approximately 2000 apartment units. Management of our own properties has let us fine-tune the process to be effective and efficient. We know exactly what property owners require. It is no surprise therefore, that this division has established a broad base of new customers ranging from important retailers to large churches to residential properties such as luxury condominiums. Property Management has been able to provide the tools to evaluate, adjust, and improve the performance of many older properties to be profit centers once again. Quick response by in-house construction and maintenance services result in more attractive buildings and higher tenant retention.

A constantly growing client base has resulted in the formation of a stand alone maintenance department that serves Emory Hill's existing portfolio of over 5 million square feet as well as all third party property management contracts. This division provides general building maintenance, plumbing, electrical, HVAC, and duct cleaning services for a number of retail stores, restaurants, and Veterinary Centers in the Delaware Valley, Maryland, and Pennsylvania. Full time, trained technicians and mechanics are able to respond to calls on a 24 hour basis.

Christiana Care Health System

Christiana Care Health System is one of the largest not-for-profit, private teaching health systems in the United States, operating two award-winning acute care hospitals with more than 1,100 beds, major regional referral centers for heart and vascular health and cancer, the only Level-I trauma center between Philadelphia and Baltimore, a transitional care facility, home health care by the Visiting Nurse

scenes. Those with contagious diseases were usually confined to their homes. Physicians lamented they had no place to send their patients for care.

Then, a group of women, led by Mary Hillyard Harrington, wife of Wilmington's mayor, began raising funds. She had a clever plan to solicit dimes from her close friends, who would promise to get more dimes from their friends, who would do

cancer center as well as a full-service acute care hospital. Another group, comprising community physicians and surgeons, launched the Physicians & Surgeons Hospital, which grew rapidly and was renamed the Wilmington General Hospital, where a full-service hospital, with a nursing school, busy maternity center and Wilmington's first radiation oncology treatment center existed for many decades.

Wilmington Hospital

Association, a Preventive Medicine & Rehabilitation Institute, plus a vast array of health and wellness services improving the health of more than a million neighbors we serve around the clock.

Roots of Christiana Care run deep

Christiana Care Health System traces its roots in our community back more than 115 years. In 1887, the people of Wilmington, Del., sorely needed a hospital. Electric street cars were beginning to replace horse carts in Wilmington, and traumatic injuries were common, especially among railway workers. Without a hospital, the injured often were treated at accident

the same, with the process repeating until $10,000 was raised to build a hospital. Gradually, the founders of the hospital bought land at 14th and Washington streets for the first Delaware Hospital, near the site of Christiana Care's Wilmington Hospital today. Construction was complete and the hospital opened in 1890.

Elsewhere in Wilmington, two separate groups of doctors and their supporters also were developing new hospitals. One group opened the Homeopathic Hospital, in a former nursing home, at Shallcross Avenue and Van Buren Street. Later renamed the Memorial Hospital, it was home to Delaware's first

Because each of these three hospitals – the Delaware, the Memorial and the Wilmington General – received the support of the medical community and philanthropic support in the first half of the 20th century, they developed into three pillars of health care strength in the community.

Three become one

When these three institutions were combined under one board in 1965 as the Wilmington Medical Center, the stage was set for the birth of Christiana Care Health System, albeit not until another 30 years passed. With population growth and housing spreading steadily throughout northern New Castle County, Del., the programs and services offered by the Wilmington Medical Center were challenged to adapt. The answer was Plan Omega, a plan that included building a 780-bed hospital to be named Christiana Hospital, roughly midway between Wilmington and Newark, southwest of the City. The plan also called for razing the Memorial and Wilmington General divisions and the complete renovation and modernization of the Delaware Division, which is now known as Christiana Care's Wilmington Hospital.

Construction of the new flagship, Christiana Hospital, began on Nov. 9, 1981, on a donated 200-acre site near Interstate 95. The hospital opened in January, 1985 and shortly thereafter Wilmington Medical Center changed its corporate name to the Medical Center of Delaware – the nucleus of the Christiana Care Health System and its Medical-Dental Staff as we know them today.

Wilmington Hospital

A City landmark since 1890, fully modernized Wilmington Hospital remains a vibrant and reliable source of high quality health care, near the center of town, where it shouldered so much of the healthcare burden for the Wilmington community throughout the last century. Today, Wilmington Hospital continues to offer the best available emergency care services and a full range of outpatient primary care services, including adult, women's and pediatric health care services at the Wilmington Hospital Health Center. Wilmington Hospital also offers 250 licensed inpatient beds, plus 41 licensed inpatient beds in our pioneering on-site Center for Rehabilitation; an award-winning Joint Replacement Center; the Roxana Cannon Arsht Surgicenter; one of the region's most experienced, accredited Sleep Disorders Centers; as well as diagnostic imaging and medical laboratory services conveniently on site.

Growing and flourishing

Christiana Care's steady growth from the 1990s to date might seem breathtaking to some. As if to the steady beat of a drum, the health system's community-based leadership has taken aim at the needs of its neighbors and produced a myriad of solutions. Among these improvements are free-standing same-day

Roxana Cannon Arsht Surgicenter, Wilmington

surgicenters, a major new wing to accommodate women's health (along with the nearly 7,000 births that take place there each year), the Helen F. Graham Cancer Center and now an unprecedented expansion to include a new patient tower and education center on the Christiana Hospital campus. The new clinical care and education initiative expands Christiana Care's acclaimed heart and vascular health program, and founds a new, state-of-the-science education center in partnership with the Delaware Academy of Medicine, while adding 172 new inpatient beds and 30 short-stay beds, plus additional operating rooms, diagnostic labs and emergency exam rooms. Construction of the two-phase project is expected to be finished in 2007.

Junior Board of Christiana Care, Inc.

Those women who worked hard to raise money to build and equip hospitals before the turn of the 20th century did not just fade away when the hospitals were up and running. As each hospital was established, many joined a Junior Board, consisting of loyal and dedicated members committed to the welfare of their hospital.

The Junior Boards have always held the spirit of volunteerism to be of paramount importance and directed efforts toward raising money and providing special services. More than $8 million has been contributed to helping sustain our hospitals since the Junior Boards of the Delaware, Memorial and Wilmington General divisions merged

in 1984. Through profit-making and fund-raising enterprises, such as gift shops, restaurants and special events like the annual "Medicine Ball," the Junior Board of Christiana Care, Inc. has provided funds for diverse hospital projects and improvements and equipment – the Cancer Resource Library at the Helen F. Graham Cancer Center, Imaginations child development building on the Christiana Hospital campus, the Mothers' Milk Bank, nursing and other skills training scholarships and the Special Care Nursery, plus motorized parking lot shuttles, a fire truck, and the Rehabilitation Center's "Easy Street" facility to name just a few.

Of course, many of the necessities in providing excellent health care cannot be purchased for dollars and cents, and without our Junior Board, these necessities might never be fulfilled. Junior Board members have a long history of volunteer services, helping patients, visitors and staff in outpatient health centers, hospital information desks and waiting lounges, as well as pushing the ever-circulating carts that bring flowers, gifts, magazines and smiles to the patients of Christiana Care.

As Christiana Care in 2005 observes the 20th anniversary of the opening of Christiana Hospital and complete modernization of Wilmington Hospital, we invite everyone to celebrate with us the good fortune we have shared as neighbors and to link arms in hope for the promising days ahead.

The University of Delaware in Wilmington
The Division of Professional and Continuing Studies

The University of Delaware has grown from its founding as a small private academy in 1743 to a major research university. As one of the oldest land-grant institutions in the nation, as well as a sea-grant, space-grant and urban-grant institution, the University of Delaware offers an impressive collection of educational resources. It is a recognized leader in the use of educational technology and problem based learning. The University's distinguished faculty includes internationally known scientists, authors, and teachers.

Though its central campus is in Newark, the University of Delaware has two locations in Wilmington: the UD Downtown Center at 8th and King Streets and the Wilmington Campus at 2800 Pennsylvania Avenue. For decades, the Wilmington Campus has served adult students through evening classes and noncredit professional development opportunities. The campus is also home to the Academy of Lifelong Learning, a nationally known learning cooperative for adults over 50 years of age. As a nationally recognized leader in learning in retirement programs, the Academy serves over 2,000 learners each semester. The University opened its Downtown Center in 1998 to provide a centrally located, state-of-the art facility for adult students to pursue their educational goals. This center is especially convenient for those working in the city.

The University's offerings in Wilmington provide an adult-oriented learning environment. Students describe it as "professional yet relaxed" and comment on the superior technology. Facilities, from classrooms to spaces for studying and relaxing, have been designed specifically with the adult student in mind.

A range of course formats and programs are available in Wilmington, designed for the business community and its employees. Traditional evening courses for academic credit provide the opportunity for degree completion. UD Online distance learning technology augments the course

offerings with classes available online and on CD-ROM, which students can access from the convenience of their home or office, 24/7.

Many professional development programs fit the needs of Wilmington's workforce, whether they seek to update skills, advance in their careers or strengthen their credentials in the workplace. Many students pursue certificate programs, series of sequential courses offering practical, concentrated study in a specific professional area. These can be completed in a relatively short time through part-time study, making them a sensible choice for individuals with demanding work lives. Certificates offered in Wilmington include programs in paralegal studies, project management, performance management, supervision and leadership, and training and employee development.

Wilmington businesses have taken advantage of the opportunity to customize noncredit programs specifically for their

organizations. University staff works closely with the organization to assess long- and short-term training needs and tailor programs to meet them. Businesses benefit from a professional team skilled in the design, delivery and facilitation of top quality programs. Customized programs are convenient, offered at the company location or at a University site, cost-effective, and directly relevant to the organization.

The programs and services mentioned above are administered by the University's Division of Professional and Continuing Studies. The focus of Professional and Continuing Studies remains firmly on service to students. Along with tailoring programs to the needs of working adults, the Division provides student services specifically for adult students.

Through Professional and Continuing Studies, the University extends its vast resources, research information, technological advances and knowledge to the community.

*S*ince its founding here in the city of Wilmington seventy years ago, Blue Cross Blue Shield of Delaware (BCBSD) has touched the lives of thousands of Delaware families and today ranks as the leading health insurer in our state.

Blue Cross Blue Shield of Delaware, initially called Group Hospital Service, was incorporated in 1935. It was a time when just 75 cents a month could buy an individual complete coverage for in-hospital care. Two years later, dependent coverage and limited maternity benefits were offered.

The 1940s saw Kent and Sussex County hospitals join the network and a program providing surgical and medical insurance, called Blue Shield, was offered for the first time. BCBSD became one of the first insurers in the country to cover physical as well as mental illness. In 1959, an "over 65" program was introduced to provide limited coverage to older citizens.

The company's name became Blue Cross Blue Shield of Delaware, Inc. in 1965, about the same time Medicare supplemental insurance and a new program to pre-pay the cost of prescription drugs were introduced. Group dental coverage was first offered in 1973.

Ahead of national trends, in 1983 BCBSD opened The HMO of Delaware, a complete health care system combining both delivery and financing of health services. Within three years, The HMO of Delaware became the only HMO in the state and second in the nation to receive national accreditation.

The following decade had significant changes: BCBSD introduced a managed care program offering mental health and substance abuse benefits, and launched its first Point-of-Service product.

Generations of Delawareans continue to look to BCBSD for quality, innovative health plans that are both affordable and accessible.

Then, in March of 2000, BCBSD became an affiliate of CareFirst, Inc., creating a combined company that now has more than 3.2 million members, with $7.5 billion in revenues, and 6,200 associates in five states and the District of Columbia. In the years since, BCBSD's enrollment has increased 58 percent. To support this growing membership and maintain BCBSD's high level of service, the company has added more than 170 employees.

BCBSD's dedication to quality and service has been widely recognized over the years. In both 2000 and 2003, BCBSD received the highest possible three-year accreditation status from NCQA* for the BlueCare® and BlueSelect® managed care plans. In 2002, the Blue Cross and Blue Shield Association ranked BCBSD first out of sixty-two plans nationwide in the area of "Member Experience." Then, in 2004, BCBSD received its sixth straight Brand Excellence Award.

Throughout its history, BCBSD has always focused on providing the citizens of Delaware with quality, innovative health plans and services that are both affordable and accessible.

To further improve the health of its members, BCBSD offers effective disease management and wellness programs, including prenatal programs for mothers-to-be, and special programs for members with chronic conditions.

A discount program called *Options* offers members discounts on complementary and alternative medicine, laser surgery, fitness centers and elder care services.

Today, BCBSD relies on the strength of its past as it looks to the future. Working together with its large network of health care providers, BCBSD will continue to strive for the quality, customer service and product innovation that has been the foundation of its success.

**BlueCross BlueShield
of Delaware
A CareFirst Company**

www.bcbsde.com

* NCQA is an independent, not-for-profit organization dedicated to measuring the quality of America's health care. Consumers can easily access health plans' NCQA Accreditation status and other information on health care quality on NCQA's website at www.ncqa.org, or by calling their customer support at (888) 275-7585.
Blue Cross Blue Shield of Delaware and CareFirst, Inc., are independent licensees of the Blue Cross and Blue Shield Association.
® Registered trademarks of the Blue Cross and Blue Shield Association.

The Hotel du Pont

The Gold Ballroom

When gunpowder manufacturer Eleuthère du Pont settled in Wilmington, Delaware in the early 19th century, no one could have predicted how quickly the small town would embrace his business. Nor could anyone have known what sort of impact that business would have on the town itself.

As the du Pont family enterprise grew larger and more diversified through the years, the city grew right along with it. And as business increased dramatically, Wilmington was soon transformed into a bustling city where existing hotels could no longer meet the demands of visitors. It was at this point DuPont executives, under the direction of then-company-president Pierre S. du Pont, decided to build a hotel and connect it to the main company building.

Everything about the Hotel du Pont was designed to rival the finest hotels of Europe in prestige, elegance and character. The plans called for 150 guest rooms, a main dining room, rathskeller, men's café/bar, ballroom, club room, a ladies' sitting room and much more – quite an ambitious undertaking for a city of just 80,000 residents. Opening day, on January 15, 1913, brought 295 invited guests in horse-drawn carriages to the hotel's red-carpeted door. During the first week alone, 25,000 visitors toured the new hotel.

No expense was spared in the creation of Wilmington's crowning achievement. In the ornate public spaces, nearly two dozen French and Italian craftsmen carved, gilded and painted for over two and a half years. Suites had large sitting rooms featuring cozy fireplaces. Polished brass beds were made up with imported linen, while sterling silver comb, brush and mirror sets were placed on dressing tables. In the main dining room, now known as the Green Room, fumed oak paneling soared two stories above the mosaic and terrazzo floors below, while rich forest greens, browns and ivories, embellished with gold, decorated the room. Six handcrafted chandeliers and a musicians' gallery overlooked the opulence.

After dinner, many guests enjoyed professional performances at the hotel's own Playhouse Theatre, now known as the DuPont Theatre. Built in only 150 days in 1913, its stage is still larger today than all but three of New York City's theatres.

During the early days, the hotel showed its commitment to struggling local artists by displaying their works. Today, they highlight one of the foremost collections of Brandywine art, including three generations of original Wyeth masterpieces.

Throughout the years, the hotel continued to evolve with the times. In 1918, 118 guest rooms were added, and the beautiful Rose Room – the French salon reserved for women – became the new lobby. Wooden inlaid floors became marble, mirrored walls were replaced with imported travertine stone and the ceiling was sculptured with carved rosettes and scrolls. The original lobby became the hotel's soda shop, while the former entrance served as a fashionable ladies' hat shop. In 1955, the soda shop was replaced by many of the shops that line the corridors today.

But widely considered the Hotel du Pont's crowning achievement, both then and now, was the addition in 1918 of the Gold Ballroom and the du Barry Room. Both are still viewed as the premier locations for weddings and social events while also providing the ideal setting for corporate meetings or executive-level conferences.

The original Gold Ballroom walls were executed in sgraffito, a technique in which designs are hand-cut or "scratched" in multiple layers of colored plaster with special tools that date from the Italian Renaissance. Thirty Italian artisans required more than a year to complete the room in this now-lost art.

Of course, the only thing as legendary as the hotel's design is the lobby registry. Through the years, the hotel has been host to presidents, politicians, kings, queens, sports and entertainment celebrities, and captains of industry. The international greats and glitterati have included, to name merely a few, Charles Lindbergh, Amelia Earhart, Ingrid Bergman, Prince Rainier of Monaco, Joe DiMaggio, John F. Kennedy, Jacques Cousteau, Eleanor Roosevelt, Elizabeth Taylor, Katherine Hepburn, Duke Ellington, King Carl XVI Gustaf and Prince Bertil of Sweden, Norman Rockwell, Henry Kissinger, Bob Hope, Lucille Ball and many more. Most recently, former President George Bush, Barry Manilow, Reese Witherspoon, Ryan Phillipe, Warren Buffet, Joe Gibbs, Jeff Gordon and Whoopi Goldberg have each been seen strolling through the lobby.

Today, the Hotel du Pont is a member of the DuPont Hospitality group of businesses which includes the DuPont Theatre and DuPont Country Club. These premier properties continue to be DuPont owned and operated, and are considered by many to be the "front door" to the corporation. Together, they stand as a testament to their founders' commitment to creating and sustaining unrivalled lodging and entertainment experiences for guests, members and patrons.

A vital part of the community, the Hotel du Pont continues to serve the business, civic and social needs of greater Wilmington. Of course, it remains the city's architectural focal point – a reminder of a shared heritage, and a beacon of future promise. But far beyond mere bricks and mortar, the small and not-so-small human dramas that occur with every new day render the Hotel du Pont an integral part of Delaware's social and economic fabric.

AAA Mid-Atlantic

The genesis of what is today AAA Mid-Atlantic began on April 20, 1900 at the Hotel Flanders in Philadelphia. Seven founders attended that first meeting, forming the Automobile Club of Philadelphia on November 1, 1900. The organizers never imagined that their idea for an automobile club would not only become among the most influential AAA automobile clubs in the nation, but also help create the freedom of mobility that shaped the American way of life for the next century and beyond.

In 1906, the Automobile Club of Delaware County in Pennsylvania organized. It later became known as the Keystone Motor Club. Then, in 1926, Keystone Automobile Club Casualty Company was created to serve the auto insurance needs of motorists in the region. Today, that company is known as the AAA Mid-Atlantic Insurance Group.

It was on Valentine's Day in 1927 that the Delaware Motor Club met for the first time. Eleven men gathered at the duPont-Biltmore Hotel in Wilmington and agreed to lease space for its Touring Bureau and offices. Walter J. Reardon, was elected president of the group. Other officers included Emil R. Mayerburg, M.D., vice-president; William Mask, Jr., treasurer; and Edwin C. Huber, secretary.

By the following month, membership in the Delaware Motor Club reached 647 and the club began offering emergency road service. Membership dues were set at $10, a fee that remained unchanged until 1973.

As the number of cars began to grow, each automobile club worked intently on local and national transportation issues, creating traffic engineering and safety programs for the benefit of the public and expanding personal service offerings to their members.

The auto clubs erected direction and distance postings and signs alerting drivers to dead-ends, dangerous intersections or bad curves. The clubs led efforts for good roads and highway safety, created maps and offered the first touring books with the best routes and information on official hotels and garages. They established the School Safety Patrol program to protect children at street crossings and later on school buses. They waged campaigns against speed traps, excessive tolls, restrictive legislation and unfair taxes. The clubs' road patrols became known as

the "Good Samaritans of the Highways" for assisting stranded and disabled motorists. Collectively uniting under the American Automobile Association, "AAA" clubs rapidly became a force for change and grew to be known as the "Motorists' Champion."

In 1965, the Keystone Automobile Club and the Automobile Club of Philadelphia joined forces to become one organization.

More mergers followed with the Shore Motor Club in New Jersey in 1981, the Chester County and Knights of Columbus Auto Clubs in 1983 and in 1987, the Delaware Motor Club. In 1990, merger with the Automobile Club of Maryland created the AAA Mid-Atlantic name. And in the years that followed, there were more mergers: AAA of Virginia (1993), AAA Anthracite (1995), Valley Automobile Club (1997), AAA Potomac (1997) and AAA Central West Jersey (2001).

Today AAA Mid-Atlantic is one of the largest AAA clubs in the nation, employing more than 2700 associates serving nearly 3.5 million members in its service areas of New Jersey, Pennsylvania, Delaware, Maryland, the District of Columbia and Virginia. It is a non-stock, not-for-profit, tax paying organization offering expertise in automotive and travel services, insurance products, traffic safety, public service and government affairs.

In 2000, AAA Mid-Atlantic began its second century of service with confidence and optimism. The foresight of a handful of enthusiasts at the dawn of the automobile age has evolved into a unique member service

organizations with its timeless vision today of "exceeding member expectations in everything we do!"

The AAA Mid-Atlantic mission of today is to deliver automotive, insurance, financial and travel products and services that members value. Within the AAA Mid-Atlantic family, mutually shared values provide the cultural cornerstones that guide the collective quest for total member satisfaction and service excellence. This includes respect for individuals, integrity, teamwork and commitment to quality.

Building on its early foundations of emergency roadside assistance, auto travel services and advocacy of travelers' safety and rights, AAA continues to work around the clock to help its members. Making things better for people is the reason for AAA's existence. This means working to provide value and quality service, including efforts to promote better roads, safer vehicles, environmental responsibility, safe and responsible driving, protections for drivers, passengers and pedestrians and enhancing the quality of the lives of AAA members. From interstate highways to the information superhighway, the pioneering spirit is still at the heart of AAA.

As AAA Mid-Atlantic forges into the future, it is committed to earning its members' confidence as auto experts, travel planners, financial and insurance specialists, safety advocates, protectors of your personal mobility and most of all, as trusted friends.

Gilbane Building Company

Local Knowledge and ...

Working in Delaware since 1970, Gilbane Building Company is guided by the enduring values of our founders - integrity, tough-mindedness, teamwork, dedication to excellence, loyalty, and discipline. With an office in downtown Wilmington, DE, the local region employs over 300 professionals.

Gilbane is a leader in Delaware construction, managing construction averaging over $220 million each year. We are committed to Delaware with a fully staffed operational office in downtown Wilmington. Our presence in Wilmington is highlighted through work on many of the area's landmark buildings and our proven local track record has earned our firm the critical respect of clients and local contractors.

Gilbane is a full service construction manager with the capability of performing all services in-house and is comprised of experienced, professional builders. We act as your construction partner to keep projects moving on-schedule and provide accurate estimates / cost control and quality construction. We take great pride in our role as a partner in building better communities. Our services have helped many of the region's foremost companies' respond to the rapidly changing nature of today's business environment. Our experience and knowledge are the foundation of our services, helping our clients to build facilities that will bring them into the future successfully.

Gilbane also maintains a strong commitment to our community through a variety of charitable initiatives. Each year the Wilmington & Philadelphia offices sponsor a golf tournament that has raised over $400,000 for various charities including: UNCF, Linda Creed Breast Cancer, Temple University, Youth Leadership Foundation, Boy Scouts of America, Bethanna, Shoes that Fit, and Commonwealth National Foundation.
National Strength.

One of the nation's oldest builders, Gilbane Building Company was founded in 1873 by William Gilbane as a family-run carpentry and general contracting shop in Providence, Rhode Island. For 132 years Gilbane Building Company, a privately held family business, has successfully achieved the project expectations of our clients regarding quality facilities completed on schedule and within budget. This reputation for delivering consistent results has enabled Gilbane to earn a very high level of repeat business annually with corporate, institutional, healthcare,

educational and commercial owners. The company provides program / project management, at-risk construction management and real estate development services, and is considered one of the most financially stable building companies in the United States.

Gilbane earned its national reputation for such notable public projects as the new World War II Memorial in Washington DC; the Smithsonian Institute's National Air and Space Museum in Washington, DC; the Winter Olympics facilities in Lake Placid, NY; the Vietnam Veterans Memorial; the reconstruction of the Union Station in Washington, DC; the Strategic Petroleum Reserve for the Department of Energy; National Archives II; Orlando Airport; and O'Hare International Terminal 5.

In addition, Gilbane has managed the construction of facilities for some of the nation's largest and most successful companies, including Miller Brewing Company, IBM, General Motors Corporation, Northwestern Mutual Life Insurance Company, GlaxoSmithKline

Inc., Pfizer Inc, The Limited, Fidelity Investments, Vanguard, and Mellon Bank.

The Associated General Contractors of America awarded Gilbane the coveted 1999 Build America Award for construction management of the historic restoration and complete renovation of the New Jersey State House Dome in Trenton. The company has previously won six other Build America Awards for the new Baltimore Convention Center, the design-build construction of Wallens Ridge State Prison, a super maximum security prison in Big Stone Gap, VA, National Air and Space Museum, Union Station, the District of Columbia Courthouse, and the Center for Innovative Technology in Herndon, VA. The Build America Award is the most prestigious award in the construction industry.

A pioneer in delivery systems, Gilbane became a major developer of construction management, an approach which offers a wide range of services from the earliest planning stages of a project to its completion. The firm also offers program and project management, design/build contracting, general contracting, and relocation management services depending on the requirements of its clients. The company is currently ranked 6th among the Top 50 domestic general building contractors by Engineering News Record and 4th among the nation's construction managers by Building Design & Construction. Gilbane is an acknowledged industry leader in the innovative use of state-of-the-art information technology (IT) as a primary project management tool. In 2003, Gilbane was ranked #1 by INFORMATION WEEK, in the Construction & Engineering Industry for project management technology. Gilbane is also ranked by Forbes Magazine as the 58th largest privately held firm in the country.

Gilbane operates offices around the country and employs more than 1,600 people. Offices include the corporate headquarters in Providence, RI; Boston and Needham, MA; Glastonbury, CT; Manchester, NH; Albany, NY; New York, NY; Lawrenceville and Jersey City, NJ; Philadelphia, PA; Wilmington, DE; Chicago, IL; Cleveland and Columbus, OH; Milwaukee, WI; Laurel and Bethesda, MD; Charlottesville, VA; Durham, NC; Louisville, KY; Atlanta, GA; Houston, El Paso, Dallas and Austin, TX; Phoenix, AZ; and San Diego and San Jose, CA.

AstraZeneca

AstraZeneca: Life Inspiring Ideas

AstraZeneca is a major international research-based pharmaceutical company engaged in the development, manufacture and marketing of ethical (prescription) pharmaceutical products. Its long heritage of innovation has made AstraZeneca one of the world's leading pharmaceutical companies.

With its global headquarters in London, AstraZeneca's U.S. headquarters are located on an 80-acre campus in Wilmington, Delaware. Wilmington is also the global home for the Company's Neuroscience commercial, research and development efforts.

In addition, the Company operates a manufacturing and supply site in nearby Newark, Delaware. The Company has a workforce of more than 60,000 strong worldwide, with over 12,000 employees in the U.S., approximately half of whom are Delaware-based.

Products Helping Patients

With 100 years of combined experience, scientists at AstraZeneca have discovered and developed several of today's leading prescription medicines – pharmaceuticals that contribute to a higher quality of life for millions of patients and to a better health economy worldwide.

The Company produces a wide range of products that make significant contributions to treatment options and patient care. AstraZeneca has a world-leading portfolio of treatments for cancer and gastrointestinal disorders, in addition to the areas of anesthesia (including pain management), cardiovascular disease, and respiratory and neurological disorders.

With its global research headquarters in Sweden, AstraZeneca's R&D organization is international in scope and comprised of approximately 11,500 employees. AstraZeneca operates ten R&D sites around the world, including R&D Wilmington, located on the headquarters site.

AstraZeneca R&D Wilmington has more than 2,000 people working across the entire research and development process. The group encompasses all of the disciplines necessary to carry a compound through discovery and development to a new medicine. R&D Wilmington is home to AstraZeneca's global Neuroscience Therapeutic Area, which has a long-term commitment to the development of new treatments in the areas of central nervous system (CNS) and pain.

People Helping People

AstraZeneca is committed to improving the quality of life in the communities where its employees work and live by forging strategic alliances with key charitable, civic, governmental, educational and cultural organizations. They do this in many ways, including financial support, product donations, employee volunteerism and board and leadership positions in support of company-endorsed organizations, projects or events.

Through ongoing support and partnerships with outreach programs such as National Breast Cancer Awareness Month, National Asthma Screening Program, Brighter Beginnings (mental health awareness), and many others, AstraZeneca helps shine a light on disease awareness and patient-focused issues.

Each year, AstraZeneca contributes millions of dollars to charitable organizations and supports numerous local community events with thousands of employee volunteers.

Clearly, AstraZeneca's commitment goes beyond simply writing a check – it's about forming meaningful partnerships with community organizations and giving employees the opportunity to shine as ambassadors for AstraZeneca.

Since 1978, AstraZeneca has helped people without drug coverage get its medicines through a variety of patient access programs. Over the years, millions of patients have used these programs to get their AstraZeneca medicines at a significant savings or free-of-charge. As a result, hundreds of millions of dollars in savings each year are passed on to patients in need.

A Partner in the Wilmington Community

At AstraZeneca's U.S. headquarters in Wilmington, the Company maintains a positive, significant profile in the community. It supports more than 100 local nonprofit organizations through a vibrant charitable giving program, other partnerships and alliances with the nonprofit sector and a strong and growing employee/retiree volunteer initiative. The AstraZeneca Ambassadors program encourages and enables employees and retirees in the headquarters region to serve

as goodwill ambassadors by volunteering for company-endorsed organizations, projects or events.

AstraZeneca's support falls into several areas: health and wellness (including seniors), education (particularly science education), arts and culture, human services and the environment.

In health and wellness, AstraZeneca supports the local chapters of non-profits such as the American Cancer Society, American Heart Association and the American Red Cross. The Company is also a major champion of senior-related programs held throughout local senior centers and senior living facilities. For example, a special initiative called "ElderBuddy" was created, in which AstraZeneca employee volunteers are matched with seniors who need companionship.

In the area of education, AstraZeneca and its employee volunteers are actively engaged in Adopt-a-School and Read Aloud Delaware. The Company's support for science education extends to providing dollars and volunteers for regional science fairs, classroom education programs and mentoring initiatives.

In the arts and culture arena, AstraZeneca supports a number of programs and education/outreach initiatives, with special emphasis on those that celebrate diversity and those that in some way connect the arts with health. Support for the environment includes an active employee volunteer committee that organizes an annual Earth Day program, as well as year-round clean-up and environmental awareness projects.

Local Roots.... Global Impact

AstraZeneca employees, local and global, are all inspired by the possibilities of medicine. They share a commitment to developing and delivering medicines that offer improved health and quality of life for patients, better health economics for society and attractive growth for the Company. They are dedicated to making a difference in the marketplace, in the lives of the people who use their products, and in their communities. The touchstone of their endeavors is captured by one phrase: *Life Inspiring Ideas.*

Wilmington Blue Rocks

Baseball has a storied past and present in the city of Wilmington. In 1940, R.R.M. (Bob) Carpenter brought professional baseball back to the city with the original Wilmington Blue Rocks. The team was a Class B Interstate affiliate of the Philadelphia A's. Hall of Famer Connie Mack owned the Blue Rocks for their first four years of existence. Another Hall of Famer, Chief Bender, served as the Blue Rocks first manager.

The nickname "Blue Rocks" came from 73-year-old Robert Miller in a name-the-team contest. Miller lived in the Henry Clay section of the city, famed for its blue granite found along the Brandywine River.

After setting many records for attendance, the Blue Rocks' fan support dwindled and 1952 was their final season in the Interstate League.

After a 40-year void of baseball in Wilmington, a minor league team would be brought back to the area thanks to an agreement made between Delaware State Legislator Steve Taylor and current Blue Rocks Owner/President Matt Minker to bring a team to Wilmington. A deal then was struck to purchase the Peninsula Pilots (Hampton, VA), who were members of the Carolina League, and move them to Wilmington following the 1992 season. It was also decided that the team nickname would remain from the 1940-1952 team, the Wilmington Blue Rocks.

Now that the business side of moving a team to Wilmington had taken place, the only thing that remained was to find a location and to build the facility. Minker would not only be an owner of the new team, but his construction company would build the stadium as well. Daniel S. Frawley, mayor of the city of Wilmington, proposed the Dravo Shipyard as the home for a new stadium and the parties involved agreed on the site.

The deal hit a snag as the Carolina League would not award Wilmington a Carolina League franchise unless work was started on a new stadium. The

Delaware Stadium Corporation (DSC), the group that owns Frawley Stadium, would not permit construction to begin unless the Carolina League awarded Wilmington a franchise. That is when Minker stepped in and struck a handshake deal with John Casey from the Delaware Economic Development Office. Minker agreed to begin construction on the new stadium without any guarantee from either the Carolina League or the DSC that the team would even play in Wilmington. After three weeks of work, the Carolina League awarded the franchise to Wilmington and the DSC gave the approval for construction. Minker Construction completed the stadium in just six months (normally a minor league stadium takes a year or more to build).

Johnny Damon, 1994

The work was completed in time for the opening day scheduled for April 16, 1993, but the fans would have to wait another day to see baseball's return to Wilmington due to a rainout. On April 17, 1993, the modern day Blue Rocks took the field for a day-night doubleheader, and delighted the 5,288 fans with a come-from-behind 6-5 victory over the Winston-Salem Spirits.

Since 1993, the Blue Rocks have enjoyed a dozen successful seasons in Wilmington both on and off the field of play. Many current Major League players have played in Wilmington, including Johnny Damon, *Mike Sweeney, 1995* Mike Sweeney and Carlos Beltran to name a few.

Frawley Stadium was the first major project that began the revitalization of the Wilmington Riverfront along the Christina River. "Without the Blue Rocks, the Wilmington Riverfront would not be the

success it is today," said Tom Carper, former governor (1993-2001) and current United States senator from the state of Delaware. "Since 1993, along with hundreds of other fans, I have brought my family to Frawley

U.S. Senator Tom Carper

Stadium again and again to enjoy America's favorite pastime. The Blue Rocks extraordinary success, both on and off the field, has served as a catalyst for the growth and development along the Christina River. Bringing the Blue Rocks back to Wilmington has been a home run for our community. The recently announced partnership with the World Champion Boston Red Sox is a home run, too. With runners on base."

Carlos Beltran, 1997

The Blue Rocks have drawn 3,956,675 fans to Frawley Stadium since 1993 and look forward to welcoming their 4 millionth fan in 2005. The franchise has won four Carolina League titles (1994, 1996, 1998 & 1999). The modern day Blue Rocks also boast the best winning percentage among all full season minor league clubs (943-728; .564) over their first 12 seasons. Since day one, the Wilmington Blue Rocks have prided themselves on being the area's No. 1 choice for fun, affordable, family entertainment. In 2001, the stadium was expanded and over 1,000 additional seats were added, bringing the total seating capacity to 6,532.

The Blue Rocks franchise would not have been a success without the visionaries who took an idea of a minor league franchise working in the city of Wilmington and running with it. The dream of having a team *Zack Grienke, 2003* that Wilmington could call its own can also be credited to the many loyal fans and corporate sponsors who have shaped the success by supporting the franchise in its first 12 seasons in Wilmington.

Zack Grienke, 2003

Photos taken by Brad Glazier

Delaware Technical & Community College

Delaware Technical & Community College is a statewide institution of higher education providing academic, technical, and corporate and community training opportunities to every resident of Delaware at four campus locations throughout the state. The college is fully accredited and provides an open door, comprehensive program of education and

Stanton/Wilmington Campus, with locations in downtown Wilmington and suburban Stanton, serves all the residents of New Castle County. It is estimated that one-fourth of Delaware's population has taken courses at Delaware Tech. Students of all ages and backgrounds have benefited from the high quality programs offered at the college. Since the college was founded

respected as individuals. The college promises hope, opportunity, access and excellence to each student who enters the door.

Graduates enter the workforce with the knowledge and skills employers need. The college offers programs only in fields where there is a demonstrated need for trained specialists. Extensive input from

training beyond high school. Over 100 degrees, diplomas and certificates are available in fields such as engineering technology, business, allied health, nursing, computer information systems, language and culture, culinary arts and human services. Other offerings include youth programs, adult basic education/GED, workforce training for adults and industrial training for upgrading employee skills. The college also offers various distance learning opportunities including telecourses, online courses, and interactive classroom courses.

Delaware Tech is the only community college in Delaware. The Terry Campus in Dover and the Owens Campus in Georgetown address the educational needs of those downstate, while the

in 1966, thousands of graduates have made their mark in virtually every career field in the state.

High tech and high touch are given equal priority at Delaware Tech. All programs at the college utilize the latest techniques and equipment to assure that graduates are prepared to enter the techno-logically sophisticated workplace of today. Yet Delaware Tech is an institution where students come first, and this is demonstrated by the commitment to open access, small class size, financial aid, a diverse environment, multi-access learning, and a highly qualified faculty and staff. A variety of services provide students with the support they need, and a nurturing environment is fostered where students know they are valued and

employers drives and shapes the creation of new programs. Advisory committees made up of business and industry leaders provide guidance to the development and evaluation of program curricula. This input assures that the college's programs are current and relevant to local employers.

Delaware Tech has earned its place as an educational leader in Delaware. Its hallmarks of commitment, responsiveness and vision have won the college a position of respect and trust. Delawareans from the streets of Wilmington to the rural roads of Sussex County have come to know that the high quality, convenience, and afford-ability of a Delaware Tech education are an unbeatable combination.

Delaware River and Bay Authority

Created by Compact in 1962, the Delaware River and Bay Authority (DRBA) owns and operates the Delaware Memorial Bridge Twin Span; the Cape May-Lewes Ferry, and the Three Forts Ferry Crossing. Since its inception, the DRBA has successfully carried out its primary mission of providing vital transportation links between the States of New Jersey and Delaware.

With the passage of the 1990 Compact Amendments, the Authority's role was expanded to permit its participation in economic development initiatives in Gloucester, Salem, Cumberland, and Cape May counties in New Jersey and the three counties of Delaware. Using these new powers, the bi-state agency established the Salem County Business Center in Carney's Point Township, added five aviation facilities to its transportation family -- New Castle Airport, Cape May Airport, Millville Airport, the Civil Air Terminal at Dover, and the Delaware Airpark, and aided the revitalization efforts along the Christina River. The economic development mission of the DRBA is to attract new business to the area, providing additional jobs for area residents and an increased economic base to the community

One of these projects is the Authority-owned Riverfront Market, which has become a popular gathering spot at the north end of the Riverfront District. The market is located in a restored historic warehouse on South Market Street and offers a unique blend of vendors. An ideal spot for people to both enjoy a meal and shop for specialty groceries, the Market offers an excellent lunch menu with a wide variety of choices. Everything from sushi to traditional deli sandwiches and rotisserie chicken are available as well as a fully stocked salad bar. In addition to dining, the Market offers many other attractions for the customer including fresh cut flowers, hand-cut meats, fine pastas, and the freshest bakery goods. "The European-style market has helped to attract more tourists and shoppers to the Riverfront," says Donald Rainear, Deputy Executive Director of the Delaware River and Bay Authority. "It is an important attraction in and of itself and adds to the overall positive personality of the Riverfront region."

The Riverfront Market is also the home of Harry's Seafood Grill, a premiere seafood restaurant with a reputation for upscale dining. Under the ownership of Xavier Teixido and chef David Leo Banks,

the same people who own Harry's Savoy Grill in suburban Wilmington, this fine eatery has become a major draw for the market and the entire Riverfront District.

The Authority is dedicated to existing projects like the Wilmington Riverfront and, as importantly, setting the stage for future development in the region. An important aspect of this effort is attracting businesses and corporations into the area

From the Delaware River bank in New Castle, a glimpse of the Delaware Memorial Bridge Twin Span at dusk.

Harry's Seafood Grill, Riverfront Market

by providing quality sites that are approved and ready to meet their needs. The Authority owns property in the New Castle Corporate Commons that has already received all necessary approvals for the construction of large Class A office buildings with excellent access to all the amenities the region has to offer.

Another key component of present and future success in the region is accessibility. The Authority has made important and invaluable contributions in this area. One major contribution is the management and operation of the New Castle Airport. It is the Authority's largest air facility with three major runways, ten taxiways, and

several aircraft parking ramps. The Airport is ideally situated for passengers and for potential tenants looking to lease hangar space and/or support facilities. There are several large parcels currently available for lease. The Authority can and does offer corporate tenants an attractive package of tax incentives and financing options. As the airport continues to grow, it enhances the possibilities for all

commercial activity in the area.

The Delaware River and Bay Authority is an organization of people serving people. The Authority's community involvement reflects its 40-year history of giving back to the community and public it serves. The DRBA is proud of its involvement in the Wilmington Riverfront redevelopment efforts and is committed to working with state and local organizations and agencies as we continue to build for a bright future along the Wilmington Riverfront.

To find out more about the Delaware River and Bay Authority and its operations, please feel free to visit us on-line at www.drba.net.

Delaware Scenes:

◀◀◀◀◀◀◀ An elegant antique carriage takes in a Chateau Country spring
◀◀◀◀◀◀ The dawn's early light glints off the Hercules building downtown
◀◀◀◀◀ Tulips in bloom at Rockford Park
◀◀◀◀ St. Thomas Church and neighborhood
◀◀◀ Charles Parks' Vietnam Veterans Memorial
◀◀ Springtime at Winterthur, An American Country Estate
◀ Ice-coated trees at Delaware National Country Club

◀ Page 225: The sun rises over a tanker across the rippling waters of the Delaware River.

Inside back cover: Christina Landing, preeminent on Wilmington's residential development scene, includes a high-profile, luxury-apartment high rise that's become a new landmark on the skyline. This Buccini/Pollen project also includes townhomes and condos. ▶